SEER

ACTIVATIONS

101 Ways to Train Your Spiritual Eyes to See with Prophetic Accuracy

by Jennifer LeClaire

SEER ACTIVATIONS
101 WAYS TO TRAIN YOUR SPIRITUAL EYES
TO SEE WITH PROPHETIC ACCURACY
Copyright © Jennifer LeClaire 2020

Unless otherwise noted, Scripture quotations are taken from the Modern English Version of the Bible.

Jennifer LeClaire's books are available at most Christian bookstores.
Published by Awakening Media
P.O. Box 30563
Fort Lauderdale, FL 33301
www.jenniferleclaire.org

TABLE OF CONTENTS

ACKNOWLEDGEMENTS

I'M GRATEFUL TO Holy Spirit for opening my eyes and charging me with a mandate to raise up seers and seeing people. So far, it's been one of the most thrilling assignments of my life. I'm grateful to my team of prophets, seers and intercessors at Awakening House of Prayer, my home base in Fort Lauderdale, FL. I thank God for Christian International, Bishop Bill Hamon, Tom and Jane Hamon and the team there in Santa Rosa Beach for standing with me during the warfare over this book.

INTRODUCTION

ON THE FINAL DAY of the 2017 Global Prophets Summit with Cindy Jacobs, James Goll, Stacey Campbell, and others, I was teaching about the seer's anointing on Facebook Live from my hotel room in Dallas.

I had no idea the Lord was going to overwhelm me with His presence the way He did. I actually bowed my head live on camera and could not continue momentarily because of the weight of the anointing. (You can still find the video on YouTube.com/jnleclaire.)

During the broadcast, I began to feel a mantle fall upon my shoulders. At first, I didn't know what exactly was happening. I just knew it was both heavy and energizing at the same time. I ended the broadcast and the anointing remained. It was a profound experience, similar to how the Lord has mantled me in the past.

I asked the Lord what it meant, and He explained He was giving me a new anointing, commissioning and mandate to raise up seers and seeing people. He instructed me to launch a School of Seers (*schoolofthespirit.tv*) and a Company of Seers (*ignitenow.org*), which I did as quickly as I could.

I'm reminded of Jesus' words in Luke 8:17-18: "For there is nothing hidden that shall not be disclosed, nor anything secret that shall not be known and come out into the open. Be careful therefore how you listen. For to him who has [spiritual knowledge] will more be given; and from him who does not have [spiritual knowledge], even what he thinks and guesses and supposes that he has will be taken away."

I've discovered this spiritual principle is true in the seer dimensions as well. The more I teach on the seer dimensions, the more my eyes open to these supernatural realities. I've gained and shared wisdom on this journey and, by the grace of God, continue to gain and share more.

Since I embraced the mantle, the Holy Spirit has also given me practical insights to help seers understand their gift and believers break through obstacles to seeing in the spirit. Some, but not all, of those insights are found in the pages of this book by way of activations. Some of these activations are part of my school, but many others are new and the list is growing.

HOW TO USE THIS BOOK

I COMPILED MANY of these seer activations for the purpose of teaching and training students around the world about the seer anointing through my online School of the Seers (*schoolofthespirit.tv*). The course is taught live and available online.

You can start on any page in *Seer Activations*, but I strongly suggest you read the introduction and the chapters on impartation and activation to gain a foundation. Then, move through the book chapter by chapter, page by page on your first run through the book. Try to avoid the temptation to skip ahead.

That's because the beginning chapters will build your faith to see in the spirit. The gateway activations will help you stay grounded and avoid error. The starter activations will help you find early success in seeing in the spirit. After you've gone through the book once, you can then turn back to any activation to keep practicing. Put another way, this is not a book for one-time use but each time you do these activations, you may see something new or different, or go deeper into the seer dimensions.

These activations are not intended to be "breezed through" in a hurry. You will need to take some time to sit, quiet your soul, pray and meditate in many cases. There's no shortcuts into seer dimensions. Don't rush through this with that type of attitude or you will short circuit your spiritual seeing.

Most of these activations can be done alone but a few require feedback from others to test your accuracy. I would encourage you to do the solo activations alone at times and with friends at other times.

When we run in companies of prophets, there can be a strong anointing that sets an atmosphere that allows you to go to a higher level in your seeing gift. Practicing these spiritual exercises with friends can also help you find quick confirmation on the accuracy of what you are seeing.

You won't find another book like this on Amazon's digital shelves. It is unique in that it was birthed through teaching seers and seeing people and by study of the Word of God with the Holy Spirit's guidance. Along with my *The Seer Dimensions* book and *The Seer's Dictionary*, as well as The School of the Seers and Company of Seers (*ignitenow.org*), you will have strong, Bible-based materials to help you grow.

1

YOUR SPIRITUAL RIGHT TO SEE

OUR HEAVENLY FATHER is known as "the God who sees" (Genesis 16:13). Just as He is everywhere all the time, He sees everything, everywhere all the time. Nothing escapes His sight (see Hebrews 4:13).

Created in the image of your Heavenly Father, you are a seeing spirit. You have a Christ-bought right to see into the spirit dimensions with your spiritual eyes. And more than a right—a responsibility. Spiritual vision is vital to walking in victory in Christ. It's no wonder the first attack against mankind was launched against our spiritual eyes.

Perhaps you've never considered this before, but let the Holy Spirit open your eyes to this revelation: The enemy tempted Eve to look into the spirit dimension illegally. The serpent tricked her into relying on a source other than

God open her eyes and know good and evil. Genesis 3:1-6 outlines the wicked one's crafty attack:

"Now the serpent was more cunning than any beast of the field which the Lord God had made. And he said to the woman, 'Has God indeed said, 'You shall not eat of every tree of the garden'?' And the woman said to the serpent, 'We may eat the fruit of the trees of the garden; but of the fruit of the tree which is in the midst of the garden, God has said, 'You shall not eat it, nor shall you touch it, lest you die.' "

"Then the serpent said to the woman, 'You will not surely die. For God knows that in the day you eat of it, your eyes will be opened, and you will be like God, knowing good and evil.'

"So when the woman saw that the tree was good for food, that it was pleasant to the eyes, and a tree desirable to make one wise, she took of its fruit and ate. She also gave to her husband with her, and he ate. Then the eyes of both of them were opened, and they knew that they were naked; and they sewed fig leaves together and made themselves coverings."

Here's the deception: Adam and Eve's spiritual eyes were already open. Again, the enemy tempted them into entering seer dimensions illegally. When they fell for this taunt and sinned against God's clear instructions, Adam and Eve saw what the enemy wanted them to see. Their end was fear and shame and ultimately death.

Can you see it? For thousands upon thousands of years, there has been and is a battle for the spiritual eyes of mankind. From 2 Corinthians 3:4 (AMPC) we understand, "For the god of this world has blinded the unbelievers' minds [that they should not discern the truth], preventing them from seeing the illuminating light of the Gospel of the glory of Christ (the Messiah), Who is the Image and Likeness of God."

And Jesus said, "I assure you, most solemnly I tell you, that unless a person is born again (anew, from above), he cannot ever see (know, be acquainted with, and experience) the kingdom of God" (John 3:3 AMPC).

When your human spirit was born again, your eyes were legally opened to God's kingdom again. The Preacher said, "The hearing ear and the seeing eye, The Lord has made them both" (Proverbs 20:12). God wants you to see, and you can see through your spiritual eyes as you lean on Him. However, many believers don't see in the spirit—or don't see as clearly as they should—because they haven't trained this spiritual sense.

Many believers get glimpses of what God wants to show them in the seer dimensions—but we shouldn't be satisfied to remain as spiritual babes in the realm of visual revelation. As we mature, we should hunger for spiritual gifts. In fact, Paul, the Apostle said, we should "pursue love and desire spiritual gifts" (1 Corinthians 14:1). Seeing is a spiritual gift we should desire, and we have to stir up and train that gift.

Hebrews 5:13-14 says, "For everyone who partakes only of milk is unskilled in the word of righteousness, for he is a babe. But solid food belongs to those who are of full age, that is, those who by reason of use have their senses exercised to discern both good and evil."

The seer gift is part of our God-given ability to discern spirits. It's time for a generation of seeing people to move, live and have their being in Christ with spiritual eyes wide open. My prayer is this book will stir your seer gift and challenge you to see where your eyes have not gone before.

Is God calling you to walk in this realm? That's likely the reason you picked up this book. Pray this prayer with me:

Father, in Jesus' name, open the eyes of my heart. Help me see what you want me to see. Impart to me anointings, and activate in me the gift of seeing for Your glory. Father, give me a hunger to learn and grow in the seer dimensions. Help me understand and navigate the seer dimensions. Teach me to walk in this gift accurately for Your glory. In Jesus's name. Amen.

2

UNDERSTANDING IMPARTATION

IMPARTATION IS BOTH a Scriptural concept and a spiritual reality. Impartation is a divine transfer that releases an ability you didn't have before. Through impartation, the Holy Spirit gives or grants you a spiritual gift, revelation or power that you need to fulfill your purpose.

I've received many impartations that have changed my life and ministry forever. Notice I said "received." You can't learn an impartation. You have to receive impartation by faith. The ministry of impartation is clear in the Bible. Paul told the church in Rome:

"For I am yearning to see you, that I may impart and share with you some spiritual gift to strengthen and establish you. That is, that we may be mutually strengthened and encouraged and comforted by each other's faith, both yours and mine" (Romans 1:11-12).

Impart in this context simply means "impart" or "give," according to *The KJV New Testament Greek Lexicon*. *Merriam-Webster*'s dictionary defines "impart" as "to give, convey or grant from as if from a store." God has a great storehouse of gifts and He wants to impart what will strengthen you in your calling. *Young's Literal Bible* translates this "to give a share of."

We can receive impartation from God Himself or from anointed men and women through the laying on of hands. Paul told Timothy to stir up the gift he received by the laying on of his hands. Timothy received impartation from Paul through the ministry of laying on of hands, which we see in other parts of Scripture.

Scripture shows at least five areas of impartation: blessings (see Genesis 28:1-4); baptism in the Holy Spirit (Acts 8:14-20); spiritual gifts (see 1 Timothy 4:14); service (see Acts 6:1-8); and healing ministry (see Mark 7:27).

METHODS OF IMPARTATION

Laying on of hands is used in the Bible to impart a blessing (see Genesis 48:14). Jesus laid hands on people as one means of imparting healing power (see Luke 4:40). Moses laid hands on Joshua to impart some of the authority he carried. The Lord said to Moses:

"Take Joshua the son of Nun with you, a man in whom is the Spirit, and lay your hand on him; set him before Eleazar the priest and before all the congregation, and inaugurate him in their sight. And you shall give some of your authority to him, that all the congregation of the children of Israel may be obedient" (Numbers 27:18-19).

We find evidence of the manifestation of this impartation in Deuteronomy 34:9: "Now Joshua the son of Nun was full of the spirit of wisdom, for Moses had laid his hands on him; so the children of Israel heeded him, and did as the Lord had commanded Moses."

Again, we see the Lord instruct Moses to make an impartation in Numbers 11:24-25. In this instance, the spirit of prophecy was imparted:

"So Moses went out and told the people the words of the Lord, and he gathered the seventy men of the elders of the people and placed them around the tabernacle. Then the Lord came down in the cloud, and spoke to him, and took of the Spirit that was upon him, and placed the same upon the seventy elders; and it happened, when the Spirit rested upon them, that they prophesied, although they never did so again."

The prophet Samuel imparted the anointing to be king to Saul by way of oil. Oil represents the anointing of the Holy Spirit. Anointing someone with oil is transferring the anointing. 1 Samuel 10:1 reads: "Then Samuel took a flask of oil and poured it on his head, and kissed him and said: "Is it not because the Lord has anointed you commander over His inheritance?"

I believe we can also receive an impartation by hearing the Word in a Spirit-charged setting through revelation. The preaching or teaching of the Word goes through the gateway of our mind into our spirits. We can receive impartation of truth and anointing sitting under an anointed teacher.

Of course, you can receive an impartation directly from God without anyone laying hands on you or teaching the Word. This often comes through asking, seeking and knocking for more of Him, but can manifest suddenly. More than once, I have felt the weight of Glory from a direct impartation from the Lord.

3

EMBRACING ACTIVATION

YOU MAY ALREADY CARRY spiritual gifts that are lying dormant because of a lack of awareness of the gift itself or a lack of understanding about how to operate in the gift. In that case, you need activation.

In our context, activate means "to set up or formally institute (as a military unit) with the necessary personnel and equipment; to put (an individual or unit) on active duty," according to *Merriam-Webster*'s dictionary.

While impartation comes from God or the laying on of hands—activation comes from a charge. Jesus activated the disciples in their impartation in Matthew 10:7-8:

"And as you go, preach, saying, 'The kingdom of heaven is at hand.' Heal the sick, cleanse the lepers, raise the dead, cast out demons. Freely you have received, freely give."

Seer Activations is full of such charges, as well as prayers that prime your seer pump. Mark

11:24 assures us, "Therefore I say to you, whatever things you ask when you pray, believe that you receive them, and you will have them."

We activate a gift through Word study. Romans 10:17 explains, "So then faith comes by hearing, and hearing by the word of God." I like how The Passion Translation puts it: "Faith, then, is birthed in a heart that responds to God's anointed utterance of the Anointed One."

We also activate a gift through use. When the Lord gives you a gift, He expects you to use it. Just as you receive the impartation by faith, you must ultimately take action to use the gift by faith. 2 Corinthians 5:7 tells us we walk by faith and not by sight, but in the seer dimensions, we walk by faith into sight.

The reality is if you don't try to see, you probably won't. I can choose not to look at the person sitting next to me on a plane. If I choose not to look, I won't see them. If I happen to turn my head towards them for a split second, I will catch a glimpse. But when I choose to look with the intention of seeing, I am positioning myself to not only see but notice the finer details of their clothing, countenance and so on.

As Paul told Timothy, you have to stir yourself up. 2 Timothy 1:6 reads, "Therefore I remind you to stir up the gift of God which is in you through the laying on of my hands." He received the impartation, but it still required activation. You can receive a car, but if you don't activate the engine, it won't take you anywhere.

"Stir up" in the context of this verse comes from the Greek word *anazopureo*, which means "to kindle up, inflame one's mind, strength zeal." In other words, you need to put works with your faith. You need to step out and exercise the gift in a safe setting to build your confidence.

4

WATCH AND PRAY

OVER AND OVER AGAIN, in Scripture, we are told to watch and pray, to be vigilant and alert. How can we watch if we can't see? A wise prophet once said, "I will stand my watch and set myself on the rampart, and watch to see what He will say to me, and what I will answer when I am corrected" (Habakkuk 2:1).

Jesus said, "But take heed to yourselves, lest your hearts be weighed down with carousing, drunkenness, and cares of this life, and that Day come on you unexpectedly. For it will come as a snare on all those who dwell on the face of the whole earth. Watch therefore, and pray always that you may be counted worthy to escape all these things that will come to pass, and to stand before the Son of Man" (Luke 21:34-36).

Although these Scriptures speak directly to the Second Coming of Christ, we must understand that His Second Coming is coming sooner than we think. I believe this is part of the reason why God has opened the eyes of so many in this hour.

After His disciples fell asleep despite Jesus' plea for their intercession, He said, "What! Could you not watch with Me one hour? Watch and pray, lest you enter into temptation. The spirit indeed is willing, but the flesh is weak." Our flesh will get in the way of seeing in the spirit if we don't seek to strengthen our inner man. Actively seeking to go through entryway gates to the seer dimensions is a discipline that strengthens our spirit and crucifies our flesh because it's a choice to sow to the spirit.

Galatians 6:8 (AMPC) explains, "For he who sows to his own flesh (lower nature, sensuality) will from the flesh reap decay and ruin and destruction, but he who sows to the Spirit will from the Spirit reap eternal life." When we seek to watch in the spirit, we are sowing to the spirit and tapping into our eternal right to see in Christ.

After his discourse on principalities, powers, rulers of the darkness, spiritual wickedness in high places, and the whole armor of God, Paul leaves one last instruction to the Body in Ephesians 6:8 (AMPC)

"Pray at all times (on every occasion, in every season) in the Spirit, with all [manner of] prayer and entreaty. To that end, keep alert and watch with strong purpose and perseverance, interceding on behalf of all the saints (God's consecrated people)."

Along these same lines, Paul used strong language in his letter to the Thessalonica: In 1 Thessalonians 5:6-8, we read:

"Accordingly then, let us not sleep, as the rest do, but let us keep wide awake (alert, watchful, cautious, and on our guard) and let us be sober (calm, collected, and circumspect). For those who sleep, sleep at night, and those who are drunk, get drunk at night. But we belong to the day; therefore, let us be sober and put on the breastplate (corset) of faith and love and for a helmet the hope of salvation."

It's time for the sleeping seers to wake up, watch and pray—then report what they see. We need seers who can see Jesus coming, see Jezebel coming, who can watch over cities and nations, to intercede over what they see. I hear the Lord saying, "Who will go look? And who shall I send to see?"

5

GATEWAY ACTIVATIONS

THOSE WHO CARRY a sovereign seer gift may suddenly experience visions, trances or other spiritual encounters without making an intentional effort to seek the Lord and explore seer dimensions. We can see by the sovereign will of God in much the same way that we dream on our beds without having petitioned the Lord. We can see in the Spirit as He wills in the same way that He speaks in a still small voice as He desires.

The Holy Spirit often waits for us to initiate a conversation with Him. In the same way, God wants us to be spiritually curious about His Kingdom, His will and the unseen world around us. He wants us to embrace the reality that we are a spirit and have spiritual eyes—and attempt to see what He wants to show us through those spiritual eyes.

Unless your gift is sovereign, you'll typically move into the seer dimensions through one many different gates. A gate is an entryway, door or movable barrier that opens or shuts to allow or disallow access. In the Bible, Nehemiah erected 10 gates into the city of Jerusalem after his team rebuilt the walls of the city. There are at least that many into the seer dimensions.

In the seer dimensions, Jesus is the gatekeeper. He is the door. He is the one who guards the gate. The Holy Spirit leads and guides us to and through the gates. On the dark side, there are demonic gatekeepers that want to open backdoors, perverted portals and loopholes for you to enter illegally. Psychics, mediums and the like enter through these gates. Avoid deception by entering through legitimate gates rather than falling for the temptation to force your way through any gate that is opened for the sake of a supernatural experience.

You can enter into seer dimensions through certain gates in the spirit world. When we understand the legal ways to enter in, we can avoid the temptation to follow some other spirit. Check out my book *The Seer Dimensions* for more info on illegal access and how to avoid deception.

ACTIVATION 1
ENTER THROUGH THE SEER GATE OF
CONTEMPLATIVE PRAYER

Also called soaking prayer, contemplative prayer is an ancient Christian practice King David understood well. He said, "I will meditate on Your precepts, and contemplate Your ways" (Psalm 119:15). And again, "Make me to understand the way of Your precepts; then I shall contemplate on Your wondrous works" (Psalm 119:27, MEV).

The word contemplate in these verses comes from the Hebrew word *siyach*. It means "to put forth, muse, commune, ponder or consider," according to *The KJV Old Testament Hebrew Lexicon*. In other words, you're thinking about something, weighing it out, reflecting upon it in an intimate way.

Contemplative prayer is a thoughtful practice where you focus on God to the point where you drown out other thoughts, feelings and temporal distractions. You are focusing on the Father, Son and Holy Spirit within you rather than the Father, Son and Holy Spirit outside of you.

In this book, *Exploring Celtic Spirituality*, Ray Simpson writes: "Contemplative prayer is natural, unprogrammed; it is perpetual openness to God, so that in the openness His concerns can flow in and out of our minds as He wills. "Be still, and know that I am God."

What does Psalm 46:10 really mean? It means to withdraw from the world, relax, quiet your soul, abandon your worries, forsake vain imaginations and sit in God's presence. As you do, you will come to know, perceive, discern and see God with fresh eyes. In doing so, you will be in an undistracted heart posture to see whatever else the Holy Spirit wants to show you from the Word or in the seer dimensions.

Your ability to hear and see becomes clearer through the practice of contemplative prayer. This requires practice. It starts with setting your heart to do Psalm 46:10, "

Ask the Lord to help you enter the seer dimensions through the gate of contemplative prayer like this, then set some time aside to contemplate:

Father, in the name of Jesus, help me to contemplate Your ways and Your works. Help me to be still and know that You are God and to get to know You more. Help me see You as You are, not as I've pictured You or as religion has painted You.

ACTIVATION 2
ENTER THROUGH THE SEER GATE OF INTERCESSION

Intercession is a gateway into the seer dimensions. Intercession is part of the present-day resurrected Christ's ministry. Hebrews 7:25 paints a portrait of this reality: "Therefore He is also able to save to the uttermost those who come to God through Him, since He always lives to make intercession for them."

Romans 8:34 offers a second witness to this wonderful truth: "Who is he who condemns? It is Christ who died, and furthermore is also risen, who is even at the right hand of God, who also makes intercession for us."

The Greek word for intercession in this verse is *entugchano*. Beyond prayer, one of the definitions is "to go to or meet a person, esp. for the purpose of conversation, consultation, or supplication," according to *The KJV New Testament Greek Lexicon.*

Contemplate that! When we make intercession, we are going to meet God for the purpose of conversation, consultation or supplication for the needs of another. This is a selfless act; a Christ-like endeavor. As such, this is a pure gate to the seer dimensions.

Also ponder how the Holy Spirit makes intercession for us and through us: "Likewise

23

the Spirit also helps in our weaknesses. For we do not know what we should pray for as we ought, but the Spirit Himself makes intercession for us with groanings which cannot be uttered" (Romans 8:26).

Many times, as you pray or make intercession, the Holy Spirit will show you a picture. Often, it's initially just a quick flash (something you see in the spirit realm for mere seconds; something that flashes by, disappearing as fast as it appeared, according to *The Seer's Dictionary*) or an impression (the Holy Spirit's purposeful action to get our attention by influencing our thoughts, emotions or physical sense, according to *The Seer's Dictionary*). Some would call this an inner vision (a vision in which you see with your mind's eye, according to *The Seer's Dictionary*).

However, intercession can lead you into open visions (appear to you like a movie or imagery acting out before your very eyes, like a motion picture, according to T*he Seer's Dictionary*, and ecstatic experiences like trances as well. Ask the Lord to give you visual revelation through the gate of prayer and intercession. Pray this prayer, then enter into Holy Spirit-led intercession:

Father, in the name of Jesus, give me the gift of intercession. If You are looking for someone to stand in the gap and make up the hedge, here I am. Use me. Give me a heart for intercession. Anoint me to partake in this pivotal ministry of both Christ and the Holy Spirit. As I stand in sincere intercession, grant me access through this gate to see images and experience encounters that help me pray more effectively.

ACTIVATION 3
ENTER THROUGH THE SEER GATE OF MEDITATION ON THE WORD

Meditation on the Word is a gateway into the seer dimensions. Jesus called Himself the Door: "Most assuredly, I say to you, I am the door of the sheep" (John 10:7). Jesus is also the door to the Father. No one goes to the Father except through the gate called Jesus (see John 14:6).

The word "door" in John 10:7 comes from the Greek word *thura*. It means "an entrance, a way, or passage; 'an open door' is used as an opportunity of doing something; the door of the kingdom of heaven," according to *The KJV New Testament Greek Lexicon.*

Meditation on the Word is a safe gate into the seer dimensions because Jesus is the Word made of flesh (see John 1:14). And we read:

"In the beginning was the Word, and the Word was with God, and the Word was God. He was in the beginning with God. All things were made through Him, and without Him nothing was made that was made. In Him was life, and the life was the light of men. And the light shines in the darkness, and the darkness did not comprehend it" (John 1:1-5).

When you enter the seer dimensions through the gate of meditating on the Word, you are flooding your soul with light. You are not in danger of entering through a loophole, backdoor or perverted portal of darkness in the spirit realm. Even though Satan disguises himself as an angel of light (see 2 Corinthians 11:14), meditation on the Word of God renews your mind to the truth and makes you more sensitive to the Holy Spirit. You are less likely to be deceived if you meditate on and obey the Word.

The Word of God is alive and it is a spirit (Hebrews 4:12). Meditating on the Word renews your mind to God's possibilities, but it also positions your spiritual eyes to see. You may see Bible scenes come alive from the pages of Scripture, or you may find yourself in a seer swirl where suddenly you are having simple visions, open visions or ecstatic encounters.

Ask the Lord to give you visual revelation through the gate of meditation on the Word. Pray this prayer, then enter into meditation on the Word of God:

Father, in the name of Jesus, help me to meditate on Your Word day and night. Help me see through the lens of Your Word. Your Word is alive. Help me see it as active and alive in the seer dimensions. Your Word is sharper than any two-edged sword. Let Your Word sharpen me in my spiritual sight. Your Word divides between soul and spirit. Help me discern through Your Word the origin of what I am seeing. Give me a hunger and thirst for Your Word and the grace to meditate on Your Word.

ACTIVATION 4
ENTER THROUGH THE GATE OF PRAISE & WORSHIP

The late Ruth Ward Heflin used to say, "Praise until the worship comes. Worship until the glory comes. Then stand in the glory." I've added a line on these instructions: See and prophesy in the glory.

Psalm 92:1 tells us it is good to praise the Lord. Have you ever thought about why? Ultimately, it's not for Him. It's for our own good and He is our only good. There are many reasons cited in Scripture, particularly in the Psalms, to praise the Lord. For our purposes, we'll focus on those that relate directly to entering into seer dimensions.

First, all creation is commanded to praise the Lord, according to Psalm 148:1-10. Second, Psalm 22:3 reveals God inhabits the praises of His people. Praise and worship attract the Holy Spirit. When we draw near to Him, He draws near to us (see James 4:8). When we are aware of His nearness, we are less aware of the distractions that muddy our spiritual vision.

Third, when we praise and worship God in spirit and in truth rather than just clapping our hands or letting our mind wander, we are operating from our seat seated in heavenly (see Ephesians 2:6) and are positioning ourselves to enter the holy of holies.

The presence of the Holy Spirit can radically shift an atmosphere and lead to a Holy Spirit invitation into seer dimensions. You will probably have to praise and worship more than 20 or 30 minutes to get to this place, and it's only as He wills. Nevertheless, praise and worship is a gate.

Read verses from the Psalms and use them as guidelines. Psalm 117:1-2, Psalm 150:1-6, Psalm 100:2, Psalm 100:4, and Psalm 61:1-9 are just a few of the many psalms in which the writer exhorts us to praise the Lord. Pray this prayer and then close your natural begin to enter into praise and worship:

Father, in the name of Jesus, help me to worship You in spirit and in truth all the days of my life. Instead of being disheartened, help remind me to praise You when what I see with my eyes does not line up with Your Word so that I maintain my spiritual sight. Help me stay focused on You through praise and worship until my atmosphere shifts and my spiritual sight shifts from the natural dimension to the seer dimensions. Open my spiritual eyes wider as I praise and worship You.

ACTIVATION 5
ENTER THROUGH THE GATE OF IMAGINATION

When your spirit was born again, you gained the ability to see all things possible (see Mark 9:23) within the bounds of your imagination. From the world's perspective, imagination is "the act or power of forming a mental image of something not present to the senses or never before wholly perceived in reality," according to *Merriam Webster*'s dictionary.

Notice what we see in our imagination is not present to the natural senses or seen in reality. Imaginations, therefore, can be good or bad and anybody can have them. But how does that fit into the seer dimensions?

The word imagination is found five times in the Old Testament. It generally refers to the heart of man. Imagination appears in the New Testament three times, and two of those times it refers to the heart. The third reference is "vain imaginations" found in 2 Corinthians 10:5 and is often translated reasonings or arguments.

While the enemy tries to use your imagination against you—launching vain imaginations against your mind—you can cooperate with God to use your imagination for His glory. God has an imagination and our imagination one of His great gifts to humankind. Every great invention, for example, was first found in someone's imagination. Imagination is part of our creative ability.

That said, with the fall of man our imaginations also became depraved. In Genesis 6:5 shares, "And God saw that the wickedness of man was great in the earth, and that every imagination of the thoughts of his heart was only evil continually." When we were born again, we received the opportunity to renew our mind, which is the seat of our imaginations. As our mind is renewed, we can tap into our illuminated imagination to see what God wants us to see—and we should.

As you seek to enter the seer dimensions through the imagination, be careful to first work to root out corrupted areas of your imagination so you can separate what is your own invention from God's innovation. Ask the Lord to give help you enter into seer dimensions through imaging scenes in the Word:

Father, in the name of Jesus, sanctify my imagination. Help me to submit my imagination to Your Word. Help me quickly cast down vain imaginations and everything that exalts itself above the knowledge of Your Word. Illuminate my imagination and help me see things that are not visible to the natural senses.

ACTIVATION 6
ENTER THROUGH THE GATE OF SOLITUDE & SILENCE

Silence is the absence of sound, but it's also a dimension in the spirit where one receives revelation from the throne room. Learning how to remain quiet in soul and calm in spirit in order to discern what is happening spirit world and see what the Lord is saying is vital to navigating seer dimensions.

In *The Seer Dimensions* book and *The Seer's Dictionary*, we explore facets of silence at length. Silence is a dramatically important concept for seers and seeing people to grasp. A.W. Tozer, an American author, pastor and magazine editor, once said: "Our religious activities should be ordered in such a way as to have plenty of time for the cultivation of the fruits of solitude and silence."

Jesus taught is to pray in solitude (see Matthew 6:6). We know Jesus withdrew in solitude to pray (see Luke 5:15-16). It can be difficult to have solitude and silence in the presence of others. Solitude and silence, then, almost always demands drawing away from people.

It's been said by many mystics and seers that silence is God's first language. Silence can be uncomfortable at times but it is a powerful pursuit that brings clarity of vision. Psalm 46:10, "Be still and know that I am God." Posture your heart in silence and ask the Lord to help give you visual revelation through the gate of silence. Pray this prayer, then draw away in solitude and silence.

Father, in the name of Jesus, help me to be still and know You are God. Help me quiet my emotions. Draw me away with You. Cause me to lose all track of time because of the peace in Your undisturbed presence. Help me see through the gate of solitude and silence.

ACTIVATION 7
ENTER THROUGH THE GATE OF FASTING

Fasting is a gate into the seer dimensions. Your fasting should be Holy Spirit-led or you won't have grace to fast. Galatians 5:17 tells us the flesh wars against the Spirit and the Spirit wars against the flesh.

When the Holy Spirit leads you to fast, it could be for a number of reasons, such as spiritual warfare, breaking a yoke of bondage, or overcoming some carnal behavior. But He may also lead you to fast just to gain more sensitivity to His Spirit and thereby sharpen your spiritual eyesight.

South African writer, pastor and teacher Andrew Murray wrote: "Prayer is reaching out after the unseen; fasting is letting go of all that is seen and temporal. Fasting helps express, deepen, confirm the resolution that we are ready to sacrifice anything, even ourselves to attain what we seek for the kingdom of God."

Fasting doesn't change God, but it does change you. Remember, Peter was on the roof, hungry, and waiting for food when he fell into a trance (see Acts 10:10). When the Holy Spirit leads you to fast, ask Him to open your eyes a little wider. Pray this prayer:

Father, in the name of Jesus, lead me to fast when I need to put my flesh under. Help me to gain a greater sensitivity to Your Spirit while fasting. Help me deepen and confirm the resolution that I am ready to sacrifice anything to see what You want to show me in the seer dimensions.

ACTIVATION 8
ENTER THROUGH THE GATE OF COMPANIONSHIP

Companionship with God is a gateway to the seer dimensions. A companion is someone you keep company with. You can be in the room with someone, even sitting right next to them for hours, and barely notice they are there. This happens on airplanes, in doctors' offices, and even sporting events.

Companionship, or fellowship, insinuates a dialogue—even if that dialogue is without words. The Holy Spirit is our Comforter, our Standby, our Intercessor, our Advocate and our Guide, but He is also our constant Companion. We have to turn our attention to Him if we want us to show us things to come.

Yes, Jesus promised the Holy Spirit would show us things to come (see John 16:13). But if we don't pay attention to what He is showing us, we can miss it. And think about it: When you are intentional about spending time with people, they tend to show you things about themselves or tell you secrets.

When you make God your companion—when you keep company with Him—you will develop a greater intimacy that positions you to see into the spirit with greater accuracy and frequency. This is not a one-time activation, but a lifestyle.

Kathryn Kuhlman once said, "Christians today operate very little in the Holy Spirit because of their ignorance concerning the Holy Spirit Himself." We get to know the Holy Spirit through our companionship with Him. Study Him, talk to Him, walk with Him, pray with Him. He will show you things to come.

Pray this prayer, then sit a while and fellowship with the Holy Spirt: Father, in the name of Jesus:

Father, in the name of Jesus, help me to know the Holy Spirit more. Give me a desire in my heart to pursue a deeper relationship with the Holy Spirit in me. Help me understand what grieves Him, what quenches His work in my life, what thrills His heart and what moves Him. Help me to see what the Holy Spirt wants to show me.

ACTIVATION 9
ENTER THROUGH THE GATE OF INVITATION

An invitation is a request for your presence. At times, God will give you an auditory invitation that sounds something like this, "Come up here." We see John the Revelator receive such an invitation twice.

Revelation 4:1-2 records an invitation to John the Beloved, "After these things I looked, and behold, a door standing open in heaven. And the first voice which I heard was like a trumpet speaking with me, saying, 'Come up here, and I will show you things which must take place after this.' Immediately I was in the Spirit; and behold, a throne set in heaven, and One sat on the throne."

Revelation 11:11-12 records an invitation to the three witnesses who were killed and rose again: "Now after the three-and-a-half days the breath of life from God entered them, and they stood on their feet, and great fear fell on those who saw them. And they heard a loud voice from heaven saying to them, "Come up here." And they ascended to heaven in a cloud, and their enemies saw them."

God may also ask you, "What do you see?" This was a common theme with Old Testament prophets. He asked Jeremiah, Amos and

Zechariah (see Jeremiah 1:11-15; Jeremiah 24:3; Amos 7:8; Amos 8:2; Zechariah 4:1-4; Zechariah 5:1-3).

When the Lord asks, "What do you see?" He's trying to activate your spiritual vision or show you a spiritual truth. When the Lord asks you what you see, set aside all distractions and observe carefully, the answer to unlock greater spiritual truths.

Meditate on these scriptures, including the "what do you see?" questions, then pray this prayer and listen for His invitation. It may come now or at some other time, but listen for it. Pray:

Father, in the name of Jesus, if you call me, I will respond. I will lay aside whatever I am doing to answer Your call. I will swiftly answer You when You ask me what I see. Help me to ready myself for Your invitations. Help me prepare for the deeper things and higher places in the seer dimensions that eye has not seen nor ear heard.

ACTIVATION 10
ENTER THE GATE THROUGH PRAYING IN THE SPIRIT

Praying in the Spirit is a gateway into the seer dimensions. We know scientifically praying in tongues quiets the mind and we know biblically it builds you up in your most holy faith (see Jude 20).

Romans 8:26 tells us, "Likewise the Spirit also helps in our weaknesses. For we do not know what we should pray for as we ought, but the Spirit Himself makes intercession for us with groanings which cannot be uttered."

We may not know the correct prayer to enter the seer dimensions, but the Holy Spirit does. Praying in the Spirit can lead you to places you never knew existed. Paul said he prayed in the spirit more than anyone (see 1 Corinthians 14:18). And we know he abounded in revelation (2 Corinthians 12:17).

When we pray in the Spirit, we're praying mysteries (see 1 Corinthians 14:2). The Holy Spirit can choose to unlock seer mysteries to us through this gate. 1 Corinthians 2:10-11 reveals:

"For the Spirit searches all things, yes, the deep things of God. For what man knows the things of a man except the spirit of the man which is in him? Even so no one knows the things of God except the Spirit of God."

Praying in the Spirit opens a clear frequency between you and God to receive downloads about the deep things of God, both auditory and visual revelation.

Pray this prayer, then pray in the Spirit:

Father, in the name of Jesus, help me to pray without ceasing. Help me not to lean on my understanding only to pray, but to pray in the

*Sprit who knows all things. As I pray in the Spirit,
build me up in faith to enter seer dimensions with
Your Holy Spirit. As I pray in the Spirit, show me
mysteries of Your Kingdom. I want to see what
You want me to see.*

ACTIVATION 11
ENTER THROUGH THE GATE OF SEER COMPANIES

When you hang around seers and people with
the ability to see in the spirit, you enter an
atmosphere charged with the seer anointing.
Samuel the seer prophesied Saul would
prophesy with the prophets and turn into a
different person (see 1 Samuel 10:6). Shortly
after, Samuel's words were fulfilled in 1 Samuel
10:10-11:

"When they came there to the hill, there was
a group of prophets to meet him; then the Spirit
of God came upon him, and he prophesied
among them. And it happened, when all who
knew him formerly saw that he indeed
prophesied among the prophets, that the people
said to one another, 'What is this that has come
upon the son of Kish? Is Saul also among the
prophets?'"

This was not a one-time occurrence. When
Saul was persecuting David, he sent messengers
to Samuel. They stepped into a prophetic swirl

they were not expecting. Read the account in 1 Samuel 19:18-24:

"So David fled and escaped, and went to Samuel at Ramah, and told him all that Saul had done to him. And he and Samuel went and stayed in Naioth. Now it was told Saul, saying, 'Take note, David is at Naioth in Ramah!'

"Then Saul sent messengers to take David. And when they saw the group of prophets prophesying, and Samuel standing as leader over them, the Spirit of God came upon the messengers of Saul, and they also prophesied.

"And when Saul was told, he sent other messengers, and they prophesied likewise. Then Saul sent messengers again the third time, and they prophesied also. Then he also went to Ramah, and came to the great well that is at Sechu. So he asked, and said, 'Where are Samuel and David?'

"And someone said, 'Indeed they are at Naioth in Ramah.' So he went there to Naioth in Ramah. Then the Spirit of God was upon him also, and he went on and prophesied until he came to Naioth in Ramah.

"And he also stripped off his clothes and prophesied before Samuel in like manner, and lay down naked all that day and all that night. Therefore they say, 'Is Saul also among the prophets?'"

Pray this prayer: *Father, in the name, of Jesus, connect me with a company of seers and seeing people. Bring me into fellowship with a people of like precious faith that understand the reality of seer dimensions and have a hunger to go deeper while avoiding error. Show me a safe place to align and connect.*

6

PSALMS THAT STRENGTHEN THE SEER GIFT

FOR THE MOST PART, prophets and seers wrote the psalms. Hidden within the pages of this lengthy, poetic book are scriptures on which you can meditate and prayers you can pray to stir your hunger and strengthen your seer gift. Read on:

"As for me, I will see Your face in righteousness; I shall be satisfied when I awake in Your likeness" (Psalm 17:15)

"This is Jacob, the generation of those who seek Him, who seek Your face. Selah" (Psalm 24:6).

"One thing I have desired of the Lord, that will I seek: That I may dwell in the house of the Lord All the days of my life, to behold the beauty of the Lord, and to inquire in His temple" (Psalm 27:4).

"When You said, 'Seek My face,' My heart said to You, "Your face, Lord, I will seek" (Psalm 27:8).

"I would have lost heart, unless I had believed that I would see the goodness of the Lord In the land of the living" (Psalm 27:13).

"Oh, taste and see that the Lord is good; Blessed is the man who trusts in Him!" (Psalm 34:8).

"Who is the man who desires life, and loves many days, that he may see good?" (Psalm 34:12).

"For with You is the fountain of life; In Your light we see light" (Psalm 36:9).

"The wicked plots against the just, and gnashes at him with his teeth. The Lord laughs at him, for He sees that his day is coming" (Psalm 37:12-14).

"Wait on the Lord, and keep His way, and He shall exalt you to inherit the land; When the wicked are cut off, you shall see it" (Psalm 37:34).

"I have seen the wicked in great power, and spreading himself like a native green tree" (Psalm 37:5).

"As we have heard, so we have seen in the city of the Lord of hosts, In the city of our God: God will establish it forever. Selah" (Psalm 48:8).

"So I have looked for You in the sanctuary, to see Your power and Your glory" (Psalm 63:2).

"Come and see the works of God; He is awesome in His doing toward the sons of men" (Psalm 66:5).

"The heavens declare His righteousness, and all the peoples see His glory" (Psalm 97:6).

"Seek the Lord and His strength; Seek His face evermore! (Psalm 105:4).

"Open my eyes, that I may see wondrous things from Your law" (Psalm 119:18).

"I see the treacherous, and am disgusted, because they do not keep Your word" (Psalm 119:58).

7

STARTER ACTIVATIONS

NOW THAT YOU UNDERSTAND the main gates through which you can enter the seer dimensions, we can move into starter activations. I would urge you not to move on to the other activations in this book until you have pressed into these. The activations on level one are intentionally created and ordered to help you avoid seer deceptions that can creep it at higher levels.

ACTIVATION 12
ASK THE LORD TO CLEANSE AND HEAL YOUR EYES

Many people's eyes need cleansing and or healing. Psalm 146:8 says the Lord opens the eyes of the blind. Jesus came to open the eyes of the blind, not just physically but also spiritually. Many have looked upon sinful things and damaged their ability to see in the spirit.

Confess any sins of your eyes, including the lust of the eyes, and ask the Lord to cleanse your eyes from all unrighteousness, according to 1 John 1:19. Ask the Lord to purify your heart so you can see Him, according to Matthew 5:8. Finally, ask the Lord to heal your eyes and restore your spiritual vision.

Pray this prayer: *Father, in the name of Jesus, heal my eyes. Cleanse me from the unrighteousness that entered my life through my eye gates. Forgive me for the lust of the eyes. Purify my eyes. Give me eye salve and the healing balm of Gilead. Restore my spiritual eyesight so I can behold Your beauty and whatever else you allow me to see in the spirit.*

ACTIVATION 13
ASK GOD TO OPEN THE EYES OF YOUR HEART

You see in the natural realm when light enters the eye. We see in the spirit when light enters the eyes of our heart, or your spirit man. You don't see into the spirit with your natural eyes. You see into the spirit with your spiritual eyes.

In Ephesians 1:18-19, Paul prayed that the eyes of our heart would be enlightened so we would know the hope of our calling. When the eyes of your heart are enlightened you can see and know many things in the spirit. You will receive revelation, understanding, discernment, wisdom, and more.

Still your soul in a quiet place. Close your eyes and take a deep breath. Ask God to open the eyes of your heart. Then wait. You may see a faint image, a clear picture or a great vision. This is an activation you need to do repeatedly, even after you start seeing in the spirit with regularity.

If you feel your spiritual eyes have been blinded, let this passage from Matthew 20: build your faith: "And behold, two blind men sitting by the road, when they heard that Jesus was passing by, cried out, saying, 'Have mercy on us, O Lord, Son of David!'

"Then the multitude warned them that they should be quiet; but they cried out all the more, saying, 'Have mercy on us, O Lord, Son of David!' So Jesus stood still and called them, and said, 'What do you want Me to do for you?' They said to Him, "Lord, that our eyes may be opened.' And immediately their eyes received sight, and they followed Him."

Jesus knows when you can't see, but often He won't do anything about it until you get desperate enough to ask the Father in His name to open your eyes. Confessing the Word of God activates your faith. Your faith further activates your sight. But sometimes you also have to ask.

Pray this simple prayer: *Father, in the name of Jesus, open the eyes of my heart. Open them wide so that I can see Your beauty, Your glory, Your angels and more.*

ACTIVATION 14
CONFESS SCRIPTURES ON SEEING

Confess repeatedly what God says about your spiritual eyes and seeing in the spirit. Here are Scriptures for your reference (below). Note: In some cases, these have been adapted for first person confession.

Open my eyes, that I may see wondrous things from Your law (Psalm 119:18).

The eyes of your understanding are enlightened by the Holy Spirit so I may know what is the hope of His calling, what are the riches of the glory of His inheritance in the saints (Ephesians 1:18).

Also read these follow Scriptures to build your faith as you set out to confess your spiritual eyes are opened:

"Then the Lord opened Balaam's eyes, and he saw the Angel of the Lord standing in the way with His drawn sword in His hand; and he bowed his head and fell flat on his face" (Numbers 22:31). Keep in mind if the Lord will open the eyes of a disobedient prophet in the

Old Testament, how much more will He open the eyes of a New Testament believer in Christ who is hungry to see through their spiritual eyes?

"And Elisha prayed, and said, 'Lord, I pray, open his eyes that he may see.' Then the Lord opened the eyes of the young man, and he saw. And behold, the mountain was full of horses and chariots of fire all around Elisha. So when the Syrians came down to him, Elisha prayed to the Lord, and said, 'Strike this people, I pray, with blindness.' And He struck them with blindness according to the word of Elisha.

"Now Elisha said to them, 'This is not the way, nor is this the city. Follow me, and I will bring you to the man whom you seek.' But he led them to Samaria. So it was, when they had come to Samaria, that Elisha said, 'Lord, open the eyes of these men, that they may see.' And the Lord opened their eyes, and they saw; and there they were, inside Samaria!" (2 Kings 6:17-20)

Pray this prayer: *Father, in the name of Jesus, help me confess Your Word and what You say about me. Help me echo the words of Jesus, the High Priest of my confession. Help me not to confess words that blind my eyes but words of life that open them wider and help me see more accurately and more often in the seer dimensions.*

ACTIVATION 15
DRAW A PICTURE

In the Parable of the Mustard seed, Jesus was asked, "To what shall we liken the kingdom of God? Or with what parable shall we picture it?" And the Pharisees asked Jesus if the Jews should pay taxes in order to trap Him into violating the Roman Empire, He told them to give Him a coin and asked them a question: Whose picture and title are stamped on it?" (Matthew 22:19, NLT)

God does use pictures to send messages. Those pictures are also known as a simple vision or inner vision. Ask the Lord to show you a picture, then sketch out what you see and determine what the Lord is saying. The picture could be a symbol that means something to you or someone else.

There is another side to this activation. Remember, God told Ezekiel to draw a picture as a prophetic act in Ezekiel 4:1-3:

"You also, son of man, take a clay tablet and lay it before you, and portray on it a city, Jerusalem. Lay siege against it, build a siege wall against it, and heap up a mound against it; set camps against it also, and place battering rams against it all around. Moreover take for yourself an iron plate, and set it as an iron wall between you and the city. Set your face against it, and it shall be besieged, and you shall lay siege against it. This will be a sign to the house of Israel."

You don't have to be an artist to draw. This will get you in the habit of recording what you see in the spirit realm. Pray this prayer, but have a paper and pencil ready to draw before you do:

Father, in the name of Jesus, give me a clear picture of what is going on in the seer dimensions You have opened to me. Give me the whole picture, every detail, so I can learn laws of the Spirit. Give me skills to draw what I see with accuracy so I can convey it to others rightly.

ACTIVATION 16
SEE SOMETHING EDIFYING

According to 1 Corinthians 14:3, one part of the simple gift of prophecy is edification. Edification means to build someone up. Over and over again in Scripture we are told to edify one another (see 1 Thessalonians 5:11; Romans 14:19).

Ask the Lord to show you something edifying about someone. Pray this prayer: *Father, in the name of Jesus, show me something edifying for someone. Give me a clear vision that will encourage their hearts by Your Spirit.*

You may see a picture of them overcoming a battle or you may see words in the spirit. You could see their face looking joyful. Tell them what you see, but do not try to interpret it. What you see could mean something beyond what you've learned about symbols and metaphors. Just share the vision.

ACTIVATION 17
ASK GOD FOR A FEELING

Beyond seers, there are what I call "feelers." Many seers are also feelers as it is part of the master discernment dimension. Keep in mind your physical senses of taste, touch, smell, hear and feel correspond to your spiritual senses.

Paul operated in this realm of discernment in Acts 16:16-18:

"Now it happened, as we went to prayer, that a certain slave girl possessed with a spirit of divination met us, who brought her masters much profit by fortune-telling. This girl followed Paul and us, and cried out, saying, 'These men are the servants of the Most High God, who proclaim to us the way of salvation.'

"And this she did for many days. But Paul, greatly annoyed, turned and said to the spirit, 'I command you in the name of Jesus Christ to come out of her.' And he came out that very hour."

Pray this prayer: *Father, in the name of Jesus, help me tap into the feeling dimension of the spirit world. Let me see what You see and feel what You feel about a person, an atmosphere or a situation.*

Now, pray in the Spirit for a few minutes and ask God to use your physical senses to show or tell you something. You may feel uneasy about something in conjunction with a thought, feel tingling in your hand, feel your eyes burn. On the positive side you may feel peace, joy or faith arise in conjunction with something you are considering.

ACTIVATION 18
PRAY IN THE SPIRIT WITH YOUR EYES CLOSED

Paul said, "For if I pray in a tongue, my spirit prays, but my understanding is unfruitful" (1 Corinthians 14:14). When you pray in the Spirit with your eyes closed, it can help you tune in better with your spiritual eyes. While your natural eyes are closed, your spiritual eyes can still see in the spirit. Remember, you have two sets of eyes.

Pray this prayer: *Father, in the name of Jesus, help me focus in with my spiritual eyes. As I pray in the Spirit and my mind is unfruitful, make my spiritual eyes fruitful. Allow me to see what I am praying in the spirit realm, show me something to come, give me an inner vision or let me see what You want me to see.*

An inner vision is a vision you see in your mind's eye. You may have to fight off images from your soul but if you keep praying in the spirit your spiritual eyes will take the lead.

ACTIVATION 19
ASK FOR A VISUAL WORD OF KNOWLEDGE

One of the nine gifts of the Spirit, word of knowledge is revelation with information related to the past or present, according to *The Seer's Dictionary*. God reveals a word or "fragment" of information related to people, places, or things.

A word of knowledge is a supernatural revelation of information received through the Holy Spirit. It is knowledge received apart from natural analysis or human means. There are verbal words of knowledge and visual words of knowledge. A word of knowledge can be manifested through a vision, angel, dream, or gift of prophecy.

Pray this prayer: *Father, in the name of Jesus, would You give me a visual word of knowledge? Would You help me tap into the seer side of this spiritual gift? Would you show me a picture that relates to information related to people, places or things?*

Record what you see.

ACTIVATION 20
ASK FOR A VISUAL WORD OF WISDOM

A word of wisdom is God's very own wisdom. A word of wisdom, then, is characterized by purity, peace, gentleness, reason, mercy, good fruits, impartiality and righteousness. A word of wisdom has to do with the past, present of future, according to *The Seer's Dictionary*.

The Greek word for wisdom in the 1 Corinthians 12 list of the gifts of the spirit is *sophia*. According to *The KJV New Testament Greek Lexicon*, it means "supreme intelligence, such as belongs to God."

Pray this prayer: *Father, in the name of Jesus, would You give me a visual word of wisdom. Help me see Your wisdom for a person, place or thing. Show me Your wisdom through my seer eyes.*

Now, wait on the Lord. The visual word of wisdom could be for a person, about a place, or concerning an issue in the world. Record what you see.

ACTIVATION 21
SEE SOMETHING FOR EXHORTATION

According to 1 Corinthians 14:3, one aspect of the gift of prophecy is edification. The Greek word for "exhortation" in this verse is *paraklesis*.

According to *The KJV New Testament Greek Lexicon*, it means: 1. a calling near, summons; 2. importation, supplication and entreaty; 3. exhortation admonition and encouragement; 4. consolation, comfort, solace, that which affords comfort or refreshment; 5. Persuasive discourse, stirring address, instructive, admonitory, conciliatory, powerful hortatory discourse.

Pray this prayer: *Father, in the name of Jesus, help me enter the seer aspect of the prophetic call to exhort, whether it's exhortations, warnings, admonishments or persuasive visions. Help me see clearly the exhortations You have for people in my life, my city, my nation and beyond. Teach me to release exhortations with wisdom.*

Now, ask the Lord to show you visually how to exhort someone. Ask the Holy Spirit for a visual exhortation for a person, your church, or a city.

ACTIVATION 22
SEEK SPIRITUAL AWARENESS

According to *The Seer's Dictionary*, spiritual awareness is being intentionally aware of your spiritual surroundings, including discerning atmospheres, climates, spiritual warfare, and disturbances in the spirit; a state of being spiritual alert that comes from walking in the light of God (see Colossians 1:3)

Jesus was aware of the reasonings of men's hearts. After He fed the masses with a few loaves and fishes, Jesus told His disciples to beware of the leaven of the Pharisees and the leaven of Herod. Mark 8:16-18 records:

"And they reasoned among themselves, saying, 'It is because we have no bread.' But Jesus, being aware of it, said to them, 'Why do you reason because you have no bread? Do you not yet perceive nor understand? Is your heart still hardened? Having eyes, do you not see? And having ears, do you not hear? And do you not remember?'"

Over and over again in Scripture, we see Jesus walked in spiritual awareness. You can practice this. Pray this prayer:

Father, in the name of Jesus, help me to be spiritually aware. Give me the grace to enter into a seer dimension in which I am aware of spiritual atmospheres, demonic agendas, the thoughts and intentions of people's hearts in situations. Teach me by Your Spirit to be spiritually aware as Jesus was when He walked in the earth.

ACTIVATION 23
SEE SOMETHING COMFORTING

According to 1 Corinthians 14:3, one aspect of the gift of prophecy is to comfort. The Greek word for "comfort" in this verse is *paramuthia.* According to *The KJV New Testament Greek Lexicon*, the word means "any address, whether made for the purpose of persuading, or of arousing and stimulating or of calming and consoling; consolation, comfort."

The Holy Spirit is our Comforter according to John 14:16 and John 14:26. And since He's the one who is giving us the gift of seeing, wouldn't it make sense that He would show us pictures to comfort people?

Pray this prayer: *Father, in the name of Jesus, help me release the ministry of the Comforter by way of dreams and visions of Your heart for people. Show me images that will comfort Your people in the midst of their suffering.*

Now, ask the Lord to give you a visual or dream that will comfort someone. You may see images that don't mean anything to you, such as images of comforting people or toys or blankets or glimpses of their memories from childhood or a happier time in their life. You may also see comforting glimpses of the present or the future and hope God has for them.

ACTIVATION 24
PRACTICE BEING HEAVENLY MINDED

Paul wrote: "If then you were raised with Christ, seek those things which are above, where Christ is, sitting at the right hand of God. Set your mind on things above, not on things on the earth" (Colossians 3:1-2).

Practice being heavenly minded by setting your mind on things of God instead of things of this world. Pray this prayer:

Father, in the name of Jesus, help me to reject the distractions of the world that would keep my mind wandering on anything and everything but You and Your Kingdom. Help me to walk as one who is heavenly-minded, keeping my eyes on You.

ACTIVATION 25
PRAY GOD WILL BREAK IN WITH LIGHT

Deuteronomy 16:19 says perverting justice, showing partiality or taking bribes blinds the eyes of the wise. Isaiah 56:10 speaks of blind watchman. Spiritual compromise can lead to blind spots that keep you from discerning what is happening in the seer dimensions.

Take some time to repent. Acts 3:19 encourages: "Repent therefore and be converted, that your sins may be blotted out, so that times of refreshing may come from the presence of the Lord..." Remember, "If we confess our sins, He is faithful and just to forgive us our sins and to cleanse us from all unrighteousness" (1 John 1:9). Beyond that, we need to bear fruit in keeping with repentance (see Matthew 3:8).

Ask the Holy Spirit to show you any areas in your life that require repentance so you can avoid spiritual blind spots. Repent of any deeds that caused darkness or blind spots. Ask the Lord to forgive you.

Pray this prayer: *Father, in the name of Jesus, I petition You to break in with light of deliverance and freedom. Forgive me of my trespasses and deliver me from evil that blinds my seer eyes to what You want me to see. Help me not to commit these same sins again. Give me grace and mercy.*

Take note of how your spiritual vision improves without the enemy's blinders blocking your sight.

ACTIVATION 26
READ DREAMS AND VISIONS IN THE BIBLE

Faith comes by hearing, and hearing by the Word of God (see Romans 10:17). There are literally dozens of dreams and visions recording in the Bible, and they spam the Old and New

Testament. By reading these dreams and visions, you build your faith to enter these dimensions. You also gain hunger to see like these men of old saw. You can find a list of all the dreams and visions of the Bible later in this book.

Pray this prayer: *Father, in the name of Jesus, as I read dreams in the Bible, demonstrating biblical curiosity, open my dream life again. Help me discern what You are saying to me in my dreams.*

ACTIVATION 27
PRACTICE THE PRESENCE OF GOD

Beyond being spiritually aware, practicing the presence of God brings you into a fellowship and intimacy that positions you to see as He sees. Many times, God is trying to show us something but we are not sensing the stirring to look.

Brother Lawrence's book, *The Practice of the Presence of God*, is highly recommended reading for those pursuing Him. Here are a few quotes from the book, which you can find free online, to inspire you:

"One way to re-collect the mind easily in the time of prayer, and preserve it more in tranquility, is not to let it wander too far in other times: you should keep it strictly in the presence of God; and being accustomed to think of Him often, you will find it easy to keep your mind calm in the time of prayer, or at least to recall it from its wanderings."

"That we should establish ourselves in a sense of God's presence, by continually conversing with Him. That it was a shameful thing to quit His conversation, to think of trifles and fooleries."

"I cannot imagine how religious persons can live satisfied without the practice of the presence of God. For my part I keep myself retired with Him in the depth of center of my soul as much as I can; and while I am so with Him, I fear nothing; but the least turning from Him is insupportable."

You practice the presence of God by acknowledging Him (see Proverbs 3:6), by talking to Him, by praising and thanking Him. Don't talk about Him as if He's not in the room with you, but embrace the reality that He is with you all the time, everywhere.

Pray this prayer: *Father, in the name of Jesus, help me to practice Your presence. Help me to remember to talk with the Holy Spirit, to acknowledge You in all my ways, and to talk about You with others. Teach me how to practice Your presence anywhere I am and all the time.*

ACTIVATION 28
BECOMING FULLY AWAKE

We can be awake and not be fully awake. You can relate to this by the feeling you have when you wake up in the morning. You are technically awake, but you are not fully alert. We see the concept of being fully awake in Luke 9:28-32:

"Now it came to pass, about eight days after these sayings, that He took Peter, John, and James and went up on the mountain to pray. As He prayed, the appearance of His face was altered, and His robe became white and glistening. And behold, two men talked with Him, who were Moses and Elijah, who appeared in glory and spoke of His decease which He was about to accomplish at Jerusalem. But Peter and those with him were heavy with sleep; and when they were fully awake, they saw His glory and the two men who stood with Him."

Notice that when the disciples were fully awake, they saw transfigured Christ, as well as Moses and Elijah. What a sight! Ask the Lord to help you stay fully awake to the things of the spirit. Pray this prayer:

Father, in the name of Jesus, help me reach the state of awareness called fully awake. Help me not to walk around half awake, failing to recognize what You want me to see because I'm not alert to Your heart. Train my spirit to lead where my soul and flesh wants to keep me half awake.

ACTIVATION 29
SEE THE ANGEL IN THE ROOM

Angels are all around us. At the least, we have two personal angels. This is evident from Christ's words in Matthew 18:10, "Take heed that you do not despise one of these little ones, for I say to you that in heaven their angels always see the face of My Father who is in heaven."

The Holy Spirit, the Author of Scripture, saw it fit to record hundreds of manifestations and encounters with angels. In fact, angels are mentioned 108 times in the Old Testament and 165 times in the New Testament. That's a lot, considering there are only 66 books in the Bible. In fact, if you average out those numbers you come to a clear conclusion: Angels are mentioned or seen working over four times for every book included in the canon of Scripture.

Angels are not omnipresent—only God is omnipresent. But angels are everywhere. All day, every day—and all night every night— angels are on assignment. In every nation of the earth, angels are among the agents executing

God's will in the earth. If we could pull back the veil separating the natural from the spiritual world, we would doubtless see innumerable angels all around us.

Pray this prayer: *Father, in the name of Jesus, open my eyes to the angelic dimension. Help me discern by my spirit and see with my spiritual eyes the activity of angels in this room.*

Now, close your eyes and ask God to show you were an angel is in the room. Open your eyes and look for the angel in that spot. Do you see a flash or light or a blurry streak or an angel in its brightness? Record what you see. Practice this over and again in various places you go.

ACTIVATION 30
PRACTICE SEEING WITH A FRIEND

Agabus the prophet shared with Paul a prophetic picture of things to come in his life in Acts 21:14:

"And as we stayed many days, a certain prophet named Agabus came down from Judea. When he had come to us, he took Paul's belt, bound his own hands and feet, and said, 'Thus says the Holy Spirit, 'So shall the Jews at Jerusalem bind the man who owns this belt, and deliver him into the hands of the Gentiles.'

"Now when we heard these things, both we and those from that place pleaded with him not to go up to Jerusalem. Then Paul answered, 'What do you mean by weeping and breaking my heart? For I am ready not only to be bound, but also to die at Jerusalem for the name of the Lord Jesus.' So when he would not be persuaded, we ceased, saying, 'The will of the Lord be done.'"

Clearly, Paul and all those with him bore witness to this word and prophetic demonstration. It was as Agabus prophesied.

Pray this prayer: *Father, in the name of Jesus, help me see something about my friend, whether it's a warning, an encouragement or something that helps them draw closer to You. Lord, help them discern if what I am seeing is right so I can develop my seer gift with accuracy.*

Now, approach a friend or family member. Ask the Lord to show you something about them. Then tell them what you see and ask them if it is accurate.

ACTIVATION 31
SOW INTO A SEER'S MINISTRY

Jesus said if we receive a prophet in the name of a prophet and you'll receive a prophet's reward (see Matthew 10:41). One way you receive a prophet is to sow into their lives.

A Shunemite woman received the prophet Elijah into their home, preparing a special room for him (see 2 Kings 4:10). A widow sowed her last piece of bread into Elijah's life during a time of famine (1 Kings 17:7-15). Both of them received a prophet's reward. The Shunemite woman received a prophetic word about birthing a son, which came to pass the next year. Read this account in 1 Kings 17:8-16:

"Then the word of the Lord came to him, saying, 'Arise, go to Zarephath, which belongs to Sidon, and dwell there. See, I have commanded a widow there to provide for you.' So he arose and went to Zarephath. And when he came to the gate of the city, indeed a widow was there gathering sticks. And he called to her and said, 'Please bring me a little water in a cup, that I may drink.' And as she was going to get it, he called to her and said, 'Please bring me a morsel of bread in your hand.'

"So she said, 'As the Lord your God lives, I do not have bread, only a handful of flour in a bin, and a little oil in a jar; and see, I am gathering a couple of sticks that I may go in and prepare it for myself and my son, that we may eat it, and die.'

"And Elijah said to her, 'Do not fear; go and do as you have said, but make me a small cake from it first, and bring it to me; and afterward make some for yourself and your son. For thus says the Lord God of Israel: 'The bin of flour shall not be used up, nor shall the jar of oil run dry, until the day the Lord sends rain on the earth.'

"So she went away and did according to the word of Elijah; and she and he and her household ate for many days. The bin of flour was not used up, nor did the jar of oil run dry, according to the word of the Lord which He spoke by Elijah."

During a time of famine, she received the prophet's reward. Since seers are prophets, you could rightly say, "Receive a seer in the name of a seer, and receive a seer's reward." What is the prophet (or seer's) reward? The prophets reward encompasses many things, but in this case, it is a release of impartation or anointing. Pray this prayer:

Father, in the name of Jesus, show me what seers to sow into so that I might receive the reward from their life You have for me. Show me what to sow, whether it is service like Elisha, provision like the widow, or something else. I will obey Your instruction. I will be a cheerful giver.

8

ASK FOR SEER ANOINTINGS

NO TWO SEERS ARE EXACTLY ALIKE. You can get an insight into their anointing through their God-given name and how they operated in the spirit. Although other prophets could see in the spirit, there are nine prophets known with a seer anointing in the Bible.

ACTIVATION 32
ASK FOR THE SAMUEL ANOINTING

Samuel was dedicated to the Lord from his mother's womb. He was a seer prophet who anointed Israel's first two kings. His name means "name of God" or "heard of God."

Samuel's prophetic ministry was marked by uncanny accuracy. The Bible says the Lord would not let any of his words fall to the ground (see 1 Samuel 3:19).

Samuel was a miracle child from the tribe of Levi and the last judge in Israel. The Samuel anointing is bent toward raising up other seers in holiness. Ask the Lord for the Samuel anointing to raise up other seers in holiness. Pray this prayer:

Father, in the name of Jesus, impart to me the Samuel seer anointing. Help me embrace the Nazarite lifestyle Samuel lived. Help me walk in the fear of the Lord he displayed while releasing words of judgment. Raise me up to impart truth to other seers.

ACTIVATION 33
ASK FOR THE GAD ANOINTING

Gad means "fortune." The Gadites were known in the Bible "mighty men of valor, men trained for battle, who could handle shield and spear, whose faces were like the faces of lions, and were as swift as gazelles on the mountains" (1 Chronicles 2:8).

Gad the seer was a prophet in the days of David and was a trusted voice in the king's life. He was known as "the king's seer" (see 2 Samuel 24:11).

The Gad anointing is a seer anointing bent toward spiritual warfare purposes. Ask the Lord for the Gad anointing when you in spiritual warfare mode. Pray this prayer:

Father, in the name of Jesus, impart to me the Gad seer anointing. Make me a mighty person of valor. Train me for battle. Make me swift on my feet. Forge in me the character that would allow me to be trusted by kings and those in authority. Make me a spiritual warrior for Your glory.

ACTIVATION 34
ASK FOR THE ZADOK ANOINTING

Zadok means righteous and just. He was a high priest during David's reign. When Absalom arranged the insurrection, Zadok wanted to follow David out of Jerusalem, but "The king also said to Zadok the priest, "Are you not a seer? Return to the city in peace, and your two sons with you, Ahimaaz your son, and Jonathan the son of Abiathar" (2 Samuel 15:27).

David trusted Zadok to watch over the ark of the covenant. The Zadok anointing is a seer anointing to steward the presence and glory of God. Ask the Lord for the Zadok anointing when you need to steward what you see in the glory realm. Pray this prayer:

Father, in the name of Jesus, impart to me the Zadok seer anointing. Make me a seer of Your presence, discerning enough to guard the anointing and Your purposes in the earth. Help me to see and steward the glory realm.

ACTIVATION 35
ASK FOR THE HEMAN ANOINTING

Heman means faithful. The grandson of Samuel, Heman was marked for his wisdom (see 1 Kings 4:31; 1 Chronicles 2:6). He was the psalmist who wrote Psalm 88.

Influential and multi-talented as a seer, songwriter, father and Levite, Heman is mentioned as one of the king David's seers in 2 Chronicles 25:5. The Heman anointing is a seer anointing that stewards wisely and expresses itself creatively.

Pray this prayer: *Father, in the name of Jesus, impart to me the Heman seer anointing. Give me the wisdom I need to steward the vision and express it in ways people can receive.*

ACTIVATION 36
ASK FOR THE IDDO ANOINTING

Iddo means "timely." 2 Chronicles 12:15 called Iddo a seer. Apparently, there was a book of visions he penned (see 2 Chronicles 13:22). He had visions concerning Jeroboam son of Nebat (2 Chronicles 9:29). Similar to an Issachar anointing, the Iddo anointing is a seer anointing that sees timely events.

Pray this prayer: *Father, in the name of Jesus, impart to me the Iddo seer anointing so I can see and understand timely events. Give me visions concerning world leaders and help me chronicle them accurately.*

ACTIVATION 37
ASK FOR THE HANANI ANOINTING

Hanani means gracious. Despite the name, God sent Hanani to rebuke a king named Asa, who put him in prison. Read the account in 2 Chronicles 16:7-10:

"And at that time Hanani the seer came to Asa king of Judah, and said to him: 'Because you have relied on the king of Syria, and have not relied on the Lord your God, therefore the army of the king of Syria has escaped from your hand. Were the Ethiopians and the Lubim not a huge army with very many chariots and horsemen?

'Yet, because you relied on the Lord, He delivered them into your hand. For the eyes of the Lord run to and fro throughout the whole earth, to show Himself strong on behalf of those whose heart is loyal to Him. In this you have done foolishly; therefore from now on you shall have wars.'

"Then Asa was angry with the seer, and put him in prison, for he was enraged at him because of this. And Asa oppressed some of the people at that time."

Hanani also played a musical instrument after Nehemiah, his brother, completed oversight of the temple wall reconstruction (see Nehemiah 12:36).

The Hanani anointing is a seer anointing to stand strong in the face of persecution. Pray this prayer:

Father, in the name of Jesus, impart to me the Hanani anointing so I will be bold to stand in the face of persecution the truth I see in the spirit. I understand not everyone will like the revelations You give me through my seer eyes. Help me to praise You through the persecution.

ACTIVATION 38
ASK FOR THE ASAPH ANOINTING

Asaph means one who gathers together. 2 Chronicles 29:30 describes him as both a seer and a skilled musician in King David's time. As a psalmist, he wrote psalms 50 and 73-83. He was part of the original tabernacle of David.

The Asaph anointing is a seer anointing for creativity, including musical expression and writing. Kim Clement had an Asaph anointing. Ask the Lord for an Asaph anointing if you God has also given you musical gifts. Pray this prayer:

Father, in the name of Jesus, impart to me an Asaph anointing. Give me creative expressions to release to people what I see in the spirit so they can receive it. Help me tap into the creativity that is inherent within me.

ACTIVATION 39
ASK FOR THE JEDUTHUN ANOINTING

Jeduthun means praising. He was assigned to oversee the temple music service (see 1 Chronicles 16:31) and was known as one of the king's seers (see 2 Chronicles 35:15).

Jeduthun is thought to have written the music that goes along with psalms 39, 62 and 77. This musical prophet also bore six sons who were musical prophets (1 Chronicles 15:1-6). He was also the father of a gatekeeper (see 1 Chronicles 16:38).

The Jeduthun anointing is one a seer anointing that sees the presence of the Lord and teaches others who to enter in to His gates. Ask the Lord for the Jedhuthun anointing. Pray this prayer:

Father, in the name of Jesus, impart to me the Jeduthun anointing. Give me an anointing to praise and worship my way into the seer dimensions. Help me see Your presence and stand as a seeing gatekeeper in Your Kingdom.

ACTIVATION 40
ASK FOR THE AMOS ANOINTING

Amos means burden-bearer. Amos was a contemporary of the prophets Hosea and Isaiah in the days of Uzziah, king of Judah.

Unlike many other prophets, he was not the son of a prophet or trained in the prophetic (see Amos 7:14). God called him while he was tending to flocks.

The Amos anointing is a seer anointing for intercession, or bearing the burdens of the Lord. Ask the Holy Spirit for the Amos anointing. Pray this prayer:

Father, in the name of Jesus, impart to me the Amos anointing so I can serve You as an interceding seer. Give me visions of the burden of Your heart and Your solution so I can say what You want me to say and pray what You want me to pray.

9

SEE THROUGH NAMES OF GOD

THERE ARE MANY NAMES in Scripture for our God. As a prophetic person, you should be familiar with the many names of the Father, Son and Holy Spirit, as well as the names of the enemy. We can learn more of God by using the names of God to stir in our hearts visions of Who He is and How He operates in His kingdom.

Here are just a few of the many names of God. Meditate on these names, the meanings of these names, and ask the Holy Spirit to show you God operating in this light. While you can't teach what you see as doctrine, these exercises will help train your eyes to the realities of the unseen world.

ACTIVATION 41
SEE ELOHIM

Elohim means "the strong creator God." When Genesis 1:1-2 speaks of God, the Hebrew word is Elohim: "In the beginning God created the heavens and the earth. The earth was without form, and void; and darkness was on the face of the deep. And the Spirit of God was hovering over the face of the waters."

As you read the entire count of creation, from day one to day seven, ask the Holy Spirit to show you images of Elohim, the strong creator God, creating the world. Pray this prayer:

Father, in the name of Jesus, show me Your operations as Elohim, the strong creator God. Show me images of the seven days of creation. Show me what You are creating now so I can cooperate with Your plans and purposes in the earth.

Record what you see. What did the first living creatures in the sea and air look like? What did the first cattle and creeping things and beasts of the earth look like? What did Adam and Eve look like?

ACTIVATION 42
SEE EL NEKAMOTH

El Nekamoth means the God that avenges. Psalm 18:46-48: "The Lord lives! Blessed be my Rock! Let the God of my salvation be exalted. It is God who avenges me, and subdues the peoples under me; He delivers me from my enemies. You

also lift me up above those who rise against me;
You have delivered me from the violent man."

Understand the context of the God that
avenges the righteous from the enemy's work.
David was celebrating how God delivered him
from the hand of Saul.

Pray this prayer: *Father, in the name of Jesus,
help me see Your vengeance on my spiritual
enemies. Open my eyes and let me see how You
will bring justice for me and those to whom You
want to minister to through me. Help me see you
as the God that avenges.*

Now, read the accounts of Saul's agenda to
kill David in 1 Samuel and picture how God
avenged him of his enemies.

ACTIVATION 43
SEE JEHOVAH CHEREB

Jehovah Cherub means The Lord, the Sword (see
Deuteronomy 33:29). The sword of the Lord is
mentioned many times throughout Scripture
and typically deals with judgment on the enemy
(see Isaiah 34:6; Leviticus 26:25; Deuteronomy
32:41 as a few examples.) Joshua saw the sword
of the Lord in Joshua 5:13:

"And it came to pass, when Joshua was by
Jericho, that he lifted his eyes and looked, and
behold, a Man stood opposite him with His

sword drawn in His hand. And Joshua went to Him and said to Him, 'Are You for us or for our adversaries?' So He said, 'No, but as Commander of the army of the Lord I have now come'" (Joshua 5:13-14).

Ask the Holy Spirit to open your eyes to the Lord, the sword. Pray this prayer: *Father, in the name of Jesus, open my eyes to Your operations as Jehovah Chereb. Let me see You as the Lord, the Sword like Joshua did. Help me understand the gravity of this manifestation of Your power and justice.*

Now look at the scene in Joshua 5:13. What was the expression on Joshua's face when He saw the Man standing opposite him with His sword drawn? What did the Man look like? What did the sword look like?

ACTIVATION 44
SEE JEHOVAH TSABA

Jehovah Tsaba means Lord of Hosts. We see the Lord of Hosts in Scripture, including in Malachi 3:17; Haggai 2:4-9; Psalm 24:10; Zechariah 4:6.

The hosts are the angelic armies. In 1 Samuel 17:45, as David was readying to battle Goliath, he said to his Philistine opponent: "You come to me with a sword, with a spear, and with a javelin. But I come to you in the name of the

Lord of hosts, the God of the armies of Israel, whom you have defied."

Pray this prayer: *Father, in the name of Jesus, open my eyes to see Your operations as Jehova Tsaba, the Lord of Hosts. Show me how You interact with the angel armies in heavenly places. Teach me how to cooperate with Your heavenly host that You dispatch on assignment.*

Have you ever wondered how one smooth stone put a nine-foot-plus-tall giant on his back? Read the entire account of David's battle with Goliath and ask the Lord of Hosts to show you the angelic activity in the battle. Did an angel blow on that smooth stone to give it supernatural force? Did the angel knock over Goliath? What was going on in the unseen realm in that victory in the name of the Lord of Hosts?

ACTIVATION 45
SEE JEHOVAH GIBBOR MLCHAMAH

Jehovah Gibbor Michamah means The Lord Mighty in Battle. We find it in Psalm 24:8, "Who is this King of glory? The Lord strong and mighty, The Lord mighty in battle." We don't see the Lord directly fighting enemies—usually He uses people or angels—but in the Second Coming of our Lord Jesus Christ we will see Jesus going to battle.

Revelation 19:11 marks the beginning of the battle of Armageddon: "Now I saw heaven opened, and behold, a white horse. And He who sat on him was called Faithful and True, and in righteousness He judges and makes war."

Pray this prayer: *Father, in the name of Jesus, open my eyes to Your operations as Jehovah Gibbor Michamah, the Lord Mighty in Battle. Help me to see how You relate to Your spiritual foes from this perspective. Show me pictures from Revelation of the Lord strong and mighty.*

Now, read the rest of this passage from the Book of Revelation and see Jesus on the white horse, His eyes like a flame of fire, the many crowns on His head, and the name written, His robe dipped in blood and the rest of the imagery in this scene.

ACTIVATION 46
SEE ELOHIM BASHAMAYIM

Elohim Bashamayim means The Lord in Heaven. This is the name used for God in

Joshua 2:11: "And as soon as we heard these things, our hearts melted; neither did there remain any more courage in anyone because of you, for the Lord your God, He is God in heaven above and on earth beneath."

Pray this prayer: *Father, in the name of Jesus, open my eyes to see Your operations as Elohim Bashamayim, the Lord in Heaven. Help me see Your loving intentions for people as our Heavenly Father. Let me see Your works in heaven.*

You can use Revelation 4 to help prompt you to imagine One who Sits on the throne, who is like a jasper and a sardius stone in appearance. Ask the Holy Spirit to show you what the Father does in heaven. For example, we know he laughs at His enemies (see Psalm 37:13). We know He answers prayers. He collects our tears in a bottle (see Psalm 56:8).

ACTIVATION 47
SEE JEHOVAH RAAH

Jehovah Raah means "The Lord Our Shepherd." We first see the Lord as Shepherd in Genesis 48:15, but Isaiah 40:11, Jeremiah 31:10; Michah 5:4 also depict the Lord in this light. Of course, the most popular example is Psalm 23.

In Psalm 23:1-3 writes, "The Lord is my shepherd; I shall not want. He makes me to lie down in green pastures; He leads me beside the still waters. He restores my soul; He leads me in the paths of righteousness for His name's sake."

Pray this prayer: *Father, in the name of Jesus, open my eyes to see Your operations as Jehovah*

Raah, the Lord Our Shepherd. Show me the provision that causes one to "not want." Show me where to rest when the enemy is prowling. Show me the paths of righteousness.

What did you see? Did you see a provision of peace, financial provision, healing power? Where can you rest? Is it in the secret place? What does the secret place look like? What do the paths of righteousness look like? Is it a narrow path? What is on either side?

10

INTERMEDIATE ACTIVATIONS

NOW THAT YOU'VE worked your way through the starter activations, asked God for seer impartations and meditated on some of His many names, you are ready for the next level. The exercises in this section will stretch you a little further and, by God's permission, take you deeper into seer dimensions.

ACTIVATION 48
SEE ETERNAL THINGS

In 2 Corinthians 4:18, Paul wrote, "while we do not look at the things which are seen, but at the things which are not seen. For the things which are seen are temporary, but the things which are not seen are eternal."

According to *The KJV New Testament Greek Lexicon*, the word eternal in this verse means: "without beginning and end, that which always has been and always will be; without beginning; without end, never to cease, everlasting."

What would qualify as an eternal thing? *Elliot's Commentary* defines eternal things as: "the objects of faith, immortality, eternal life, the crown of righteousness, the beatific vision."

Pray this prayer: *Father, in the name of Jesus, show me eternal things. Show me the eternal rewards I have earned. Show me the eternal dwelling of God in Zion (see Psalm 132:13). Show me the house not made with hands, eternal in the heavens (see 2 Corinthians 5:1). Show me the eternal weight of glory (see 2 Corinthians 4:17).*

Record what you see. Did it surprise you?

ACTIVATION 49
SEE WHAT YOU ARE PRAYING IN THE SPIRIT

Romans 8:26-27 assures us, "Likewise the Spirit also helps in our weaknesses. For we do not know what we should pray for as we ought, but the Spirit Himself makes intercession for us with groanings which cannot be uttered. Now He who searches the hearts knows what the mind of the Spirit is, because He makes intercession for the saints according to the will of God."

We have relegated the gift of interpretation of tongues listed in 1 Corinthians 14 as auditory only. Why limit God? God can show you images of what you are praying and the impact of those prayers in the seer dimensions.

Pray this prayer: *Father, in the name of Jesus, show me what I am praying in the Spirit. Show me how my Holy Spirit-inspired prayers are changing situations. Show me the impact and outcome of my prayers.*

ACTIVATION 50
SEE SOMEONE'S MANTLE

A mantle represents an anointing. When Elijah called Elisha to be his protegee, he walked by and threw his mantle upon him (1 Kings 19:19). Mantles come in different colors, shapes and sizes. There are mantles of grief, mantles of joy, mantles of a servant, mantles of power and the like.

Pray this prayer: *Father, in the name of Jesus, would You let me see my mantle? Would You let me see the mantles of other people so I can encourage them, strengthen them or otherwise minister to them?*

Now, take note of the colors, as colors are always significant in the Bible. Pay close attention. Sometimes you'll see the damage on someone's mantle from an enemy attack.

ACTIVATION 51
SEE SPIRITUAL WEAPONS

1 Corinthians 10:4-6 reveals, "For the weapons of our warfare are not carnal but mighty in God for pulling down strongholds, casting down arguments and every high thing that exalts itself against the knowledge of God, bringing every thought into captivity to the obedience of Christ, and being ready to punish all disobedience when your obedience is fulfilled."

If the weapons are not flesh and blood weapons, that means they are spiritual weapons and you can see them in the spirt realm. Weapons in the Bible include swords, slings, knives, spears.

Pray this prayer: *Father, in the name of Jesus, show me my spiritual weapons. Show me the spiritual weapons of others. Help me see the weapons of warfare, which are not carnal but mighty in You. Teach me how to wield these weapons and show me the outcome in the spirit when I wield these weapons expertly by Your grace.*

This will build your faith when you set out to do spiritual warfare. This is important because seers and seeing people endure plenty of warfare.

ACTIVATION 52
SEE THE HEAVENS OPENED

In Acts 7:55-56, we read the account of Stephen's death at the hand of the religious system who denied Christ: "But he, being full of the Holy Spirit, gazed into heaven and saw the glory of God, and Jesus standing at the right hand of God, and said, 'Look! I see the heavens opened and the Son of Man standing at the right hand of God!'"

As Stephen was being stoned, he didn't keep his eyes on his persecutors. Instead, he gazed into heaven and saw the glory of God. As he kept his eyes off the problem and onto the solution, the heavens opened and he saw Jesus. This is a profound lesson.

Pray this prayer: *Father, in the name of Jesus, open the heavens over my life and open my eyes to see heavenly scenes. Help me to stop paying so much attention to the obstacles of this age and the persecution of my peers and teach me to keep my gaze on heaven.*

Now, start gazing into heaven and expect to see the glory of God. Expect to see Jesus standing at the right hand of God. Only God can open the heavenly dimension to you, but you can ask and keep on asking through this exercise.

ACTIVATION 53
SEE INTO THE ANGELIC DIMENSION

Angels are all around us—and God can allow you to see them if He chooses. In Numbers 22:31 we read: "Then the Lord opened Balaam's eyes, and he saw the Angel of the Lord standing in the way with His drawn sword in His hand; and he bowed his head and fell flat on his face." This Scripture refers to the Angel of the Lord, which is the pre-incarnate Jesus.

Pray this prayer: *Father, in the name of Jesus, open my eyes to the angelic realm. Show me the seraphim. Show me the cherubim. Show me the archangels. Show me other spiritual beings that my eyes have never seen before.*

Now, start looking. If God can open the eyes of a wayward prophet to the angelic dimension, He can open your eyes also. Close your eyes and look. Record what you see.

ACTIVATION 54
SEEING WORDS IN THE SPIRIT

During Belshazzar's feast, there appeared from the spirit realm handwriting on the wall. The words read: MENE, MENE, TEKEL, UPHARSIN. Daniel 5:5-7 gives us insight:

"Immediately fingers of a man's hand appeared and wrote opposite the lampstand on the plaster of the wall of the king's palace. And the king saw the back of the hand that wrote. Then the king's countenance was changed, and his thoughts troubled him, so that the joints of his loins were loosed, and his knees struck against one another.

"The king cried aloud to bring in the astrologers, the Chaldeans, and the soothsayers. And the king spoke and said to the wise men of Babylon, "Whoever shall read this writing and show me its interpretation shall be clothed with scarlet and have a chain of gold about his neck and shall be the third ruler in the kingdom."

Pray this prayer: *Father, in the name of Jesus, would You show me words in the spirit that unlock mysteries? Would You show me words that relate to the lives of people I am ministering to? Would You give me the interpretation of obscure words with ancient meanings that I see but do not understand?*

As Daniel 5 shows, not all words you see in the spirit will immediately mean something to you. You must search out the interpretation. God has the interpretation. Keep asking and studying to show yourself approved when you don't understand the words you see in the spirit.

ACTIVATION 55
SEE GOD'S GLORY

The glory of the Lord is visible in the spirit realm. The Bible tells us in Ezekiel 1:26-28 what the glory of the Lord looks like:

"And above the firmament over their heads was the likeness of a throne, in appearance like a sapphire stone; on the likeness of the throne was a likeness with the appearance of a man high above it. Also from the appearance of His waist and upward I saw, as it were, the color of amber with the appearance of fire all around within it; and from the appearance of His waist and downward I saw, as it were, the appearance of fire with brightness all around. Like the appearance of a rainbow in a cloud on a rainy day, so was the appearance of the brightness all around it. This was the appearance of the likeness of the glory of the Lord."

In Exodus 33:18, Moses asked God: "Please, show me Your glory." And Moses saw the glory. Ask God to, please, show you His glory. Pray this prayer:

Father, in the name of Jesus, please, show me Your glory. Let me see Your goodness and Your good plans for the lives of people, cities and nations. Open my eyes to the glory realms where

You dwell with Your holy angels. Again, God, show me Your glory.

ACTIVATION 56
SEE SOMEONE'S RANK IN THE SPIRIT

There is rank in the kingdom. When angels are in ranks, for example, with thrones, dominions, rulers and powers, among other rankings (see Colossians 1:6). The demons are also in ranks, with principalities at the top (see Ephesians 4:11). The spirit world is organized much like an army in the natural realm.

1 Chronicles 17:17, King David said: "And yet this was a small thing in Your sight, O God; and You have also spoken of Your servant's house for a great while to come, and have regarded me according to the rank of a man of high degree, O Lord God." And in Genesis 41:41 we see Joseph had rank, "And Pharaoh said to Joseph, "See, I have set you over all the land of Egypt."

Pray this prayer, *Father in the name of Jesus, would You show me my ranking in the spirit? Would You show me the ranking of my pastors and my friends? Help me see their authority in the spirit realm so I can appreciate and honor them, and cover them in prayer when they are weak.*

ACTIVATION 57
SEE THE GIFT OF GOD IN SOMEONE

In John 4:10, Jesus told the woman at the well, "If you knew the gift of God, and who it is who says to you, 'Give Me a drink,' you would have asked Him, and He would have given you living water."

Jesus could see the gifts in people. Most people find it easier to see the flaws or the dirt because they manifest outwardly. Sometimes gifts in people are buried under the dirt. You have to see them on the inside of a person so you can call them forth.

Pray this prayer; *Father, in the name of Jesus, help me see Your gifts in people. In an age where so many are struggling with purpose, help me minister to the hearts of people by identifying the gift within them that they may not see through their fears, pains and frustrations.*

Now, practice intentionally looking for the gift of God in people you come across. Ask Him in each instance to show you the gift. Only share when appropriate. Remember, everything you see is not to be immediately shared.

ACTIVATION 58
SEE INTO THE DEMONIC DIMENSION

The demonic dimension is real. While I would not recommend asking the Holy Spirit to show you hell as this is a terrifying sight, it can be helpful to see into the demonic realm to discover the plots of the enemy and recognize enemy forces eye to eye. This is related to but different than the discerning of spirits.

We know Jesus saw Satan fall like lightning (see Luke 10:18). John saw a vision of unclean spirits in Revelation 16:13. Pray this prayer:

Father, in the name of Jesus, open my eyes to see into the demonic dimension so I can combat the wicked powers working against Your will. Give me a visual of the dark side so I don't beat the air but rather pray intelligently.

ACTIVATION 59
SEE THE WAR IN THE HEAVENS

We know there is a raging war in the second heavens. Along with the Daniel 10 account of the Prince of Persia battling Michael the warring archangel and the account in 2 Kings 17-20, one of the best pictures we have of this reality is Revelation 12:7-9:

"And war broke out in heaven: Michael and his angels fought with the dragon; and the dragon and his angels fought, but they did not prevail, nor was a place found for them in heaven any longer. So the great dragon was cast out, that serpent of old, called the Devil and Satan, who deceives the whole world; he was cast to the earth, and his angels were cast out with him."

Pray this prayer: *Father, in the name of Jesus, would You let me see the war in the second heaven? Show me the raging war through the lens of victory. Let me see the angels fighting against the demon powers thwarting me or someone else so I release more accurate intercession.*

ACTIVATION 60
SEE WHAT GOD HAS PREPARED FOR SOMEONE

In 1 Corinthians 2:9-10, Paul writes, "But as it is written: 'Eye has not seen, nor ear heard, nor have entered into the heart of man the things which God has prepared for those who love Him. But God hath revealed them unto us by his Spirit...'"

God can and does reveal things He has prepared for us according to His timing. However, sometimes we do not know of His plans because we neglect to ask, seek and knock.

Pray this prayer: *Father, in the name of Jesus, show me what You have prepared for me in this next season. Show me what You have made ready and make me ready. Show me what You have prepared for someone else so I can encourage them prophetically to cooperate with Your preparation process.*

When you are with people, actively ask God to show you these things. You activate this dimension of sight, and others, by practicing.

ACTIVATION 61
SEE THE SPIRITUAL BEINGS IN THE ROOM

The gift of discerning of spirits listed in 1 Corinthians 12 is a large part of the seer dimensions. Some discerners discern through hearing, some through feeling and other through sight or through feeling.

Discerning of spirits is insight into the spirit world, according to *The Seer's Dictionary*. It is to discern or perceive a spirit or activity in the spirit realm. It is more than man's wisdom or common sense or criticism. We must not only discern evil spirits but also the Holy Spirit and angels. Pray this prayer:

Father, in the name of Jesus, help me discern the spirits in the room using the gift of discerning of spirits through visual revelation. Show me the angels, demons and other spiritual beings the spirits in the room.

Now, close your eyes and look into the spirit. What do you see? You could see some strange creatures like Ezekiel did. Remember, there are many spiritual beings beyond angels and demons.

ACTIVATION 62
SEE ACCURSED OBJECTS

In Deuteronomy 7:25-26, the Lord says, "You shall burn the carved images of their gods with fire; you shall not covet the silver or gold that is on them, nor take it for yourselves, lest you be snared by it; for it is an abomination to the Lord your God. Nor shall you bring an abomination into your house, lest you be doomed to destruction like it. You shall utterly detest it and utterly abhor it, for it is an accursed thing."

Pray this prayer: *Father, in the name of Jesus, show me anything in my house that doesn't belong there that could be polluting my spiritual environment. Show me items, altars, points of contacts and other cursed objects in my car, my workplace, and my church.*

Now, look around your home with your spiritual eyes open. You may find toys or books with owls, snakes, or rats, which represent unclean spirits. Do a clean sweep of your home.

ACTIVATION 63
SEE WHAT GOD HAS GIVEN YOU

Genesis 2:19, "See, I have given you every plant yielding seed which is on the face of all the earth and every tree which has fruit yielding seed. It shall be food for you."

God wants you to see what He has given you, whether that's an anointing, provision, a new opportunity, or joy unspeakable and full of glory. Many times, we don't see what we carry in the spirit so we don't tap into the potential of what God has given us.

Pray this prayer: *Father, in the name of Jesus, show me what You have given me in the realm of the spirit. Show me the doors You have opened to me. Show me where the provision lies. Show me where to sow my next seed to unlock my harvest.*

11

SEE THE PARABLES

JESUS SAID, "I will open My mouth in parables; I will utter things kept secret from the foundation of the world" (Matthew 13:35). Jesus used parables to illustrate us kingdom dynamics. The Holy Spirit often uses visual parables to show us a truth in the seer dimensions.

Consider the conversation between Jeremiah and God in Jeremiah 1: "The word of the Lord came to me the second time, saying, 'What do you see?' Jeremiah answered, 'I see a boiling pot, and it is facing away from the north.' Then the Lord said to me: 'Out of the north calamity shall break forth on all the inhabitants of the land.'"

God could have just told Jeremiah that from the get-go, but chose to give him a parabolic vision that illustrated the intensity of His point first. The Holy Spirit is still speaking to seers this way today.

There are many parables throughout the Bible with which you can practice parabolic vision. Meditate on these to activate your parabolic sight. In some cases, you'll need to pull out your Bible to read the entire reference.

ACTIVATION 64
SEE WHAT DEFILES A PERSON

In *The Parable of Man* in Mark 7:14-23, Jesus said, "Hear Me, everyone, and understand: There is nothing that enters a man from outside which can defile him; but the things which come out of him, those are the things that defile a man. If anyone has ears to hear, let him hear!'

"When He had entered a house away from the crowd, His disciples asked Him concerning the parable. So He said to them, 'Are you thus without understanding also? Do you not perceive that whatever enters a man from outside cannot defile him, because it does not enter his heart but his stomach, and is eliminated, thus purifying all foods?'

"He went on: 'What comes out of a person is what defiles them. For it is from within, out of a person's heart, that evil thoughts come—sexual immorality, theft, murder, adultery, greed, malice, deceit, lewdness, envy, slander, arrogance and folly. All these evils come from inside and defile a person.'"

Father, in the name of Jesus, show me what has defiled someone, or what has defiled me. Show me what is coming out of someone's heart that is defiling their personality and hindering their destiny so I can make intercession.

You should start by looking at your own heart. But you can look at Hollywood actors or pop stars who do not know the Lord from the privacy of your own home. Listen to their words to see the spirit that is defiling their hearts. Then pray for them.

ACTIVATION 65
SEE THE SIGNS OF THE TIMES

In *The Parable of the Budding Fig Tree* in Mark 13:28-33, Jesus said: "Now learn this parable from the fig tree: When its branch has already become tender, and puts forth leaves, you know that summer is near. So you also, when you see these things happening, know that it is near—at the doors!

"Assuredly, I say to you, this generation will by no means pass away till all these things take place. Heaven and earth will pass away, but My words will by no means pass away. But of that day and hour no one knows, not even the angels in heaven, nor the Son, but only the Father. Take heed, watch and pray; for you do not know when the time is."

Pray this prayer: *Father, in the name of Jesus, help me see the signs of the times through natural phenomenon. Show me how creation is groaning as in pains of childbirth according to Romans 8:22. Help me understand what I am seeing and how to pray for Your perfect will.*

Of course, no one knows when Christ is coming back, but as a seer God can speak to you through nature about the closeness of the hour.

ACTIVATION 66
SEE THE PARABLE OF SATAN AS A ROARING LION

Peter used a parable concerning the enemy. In 1 Peter 5:8, (AMPC), he wrote, "Be well balanced (temperate, sober of mind), be vigilant and cautious at all times; for that enemy of yours, the devil, roams around like a lion roaring [in fierce hunger], seeking someone to seize upon and devour."

Pray this prayer: *Father, in the name of Jesus, show me where the enemy is roaming and whom he is seeking to devour. Show me the devil's devices and maneuvers before He makes them so I can thwart the enemy with prophetic intercession using the Amos anointing.*

Do this exercise at the first signal of enemy interference. Don't wait until the lion pounces. Start looking in the spirit immediately upon seeing the enemy's work or sensing his presence.

ACTIVATION 67
SEE THE PARABLE OF THE TARES AND THE WHEAT

In *The Parable of the Tares and the Wheat* in Matthew 13:24-26, Jesus said, "The kingdom of heaven is like a man who sowed good seed in his field; but while men slept, his enemy came and sowed tares among the wheat and went his way. But when the grain had sprouted and produced a crop, then the tares also appeared."

Pray this prayer: *Father, in the name of Jesus, show me the tares—the false spirits, the seeds the enemy sowed that are sprouting, the error in the church. Show me the specific seed, what lies the enemy watered it with, and where it was sown.*

Do this exercise when you discern the enemy has sown seeds in your heart or someone else's. Once you gain the prophetic intelligence, actively root the seed out, tear it down, destroy and overthrown it with the fire of God, according to Jeremiah 1:10. Then plant the Word of God it its place.

12

SEE VIVID BIBLE SCENES

THE SCENES WE READ in the Bible are often epic. That's one reason why moviemakers seek to bring the Scripture to life on the Silver Screen. In these activations, we want to seek the Lord to open our eyes and practice seeing Bible scenes. Only He can show you the dramatic pictures from the pages of the Bible. But we can also use our redeemed imagination to picture it to warm up our seer eyes. You can do this same exercise with any passage of Scripture that depicts an event or encounter. Here are a few to get you started:

ACTIVATION 68
SEE ELIJAH'S SHOWDOWN WITH FALSE PROPHETS

In 1 Kings 18:19-49 (NKJV), we read the account of Elijah's showdown with the false prophets. Read the account:

"'Now therefore, send and gather all Israel to me on Mount Carmel, the four hundred and fifty prophets of Baal, and the four hundred prophets of Asherah, who eat at Jezebel's table.'

"So Ahab sent for all the children of Israel, and gathered the prophets together on Mount Carmel. And Elijah came to all the people, and said, 'How long will you falter between two opinions? If the Lord is God, follow Him; but if Baal, follow him.' But the people answered him not a word.

"Then Elijah said to the people, 'I alone am left a prophet of the Lord; but Baal's prophets are four hundred and fifty men. Therefore let them give us two bulls; and let them choose one bull for themselves, cut it in pieces, and lay it on the wood, but put no fire under it; and I will prepare the other bull, and lay it on the wood, but put no fire under it. Then you call on the name of your gods, and I will call on the name of the Lord; and the God who answers by fire, He is God.'

"So all the people answered and said, 'It is well spoken.'

"Now Elijah said to the prophets of Baal, 'Choose one bull for yourselves and prepare it first, for you are many; and call on the name of your god, but put no fire under it.'

"So they took the bull which was given them, and they prepared it, and called on the name of Baal from morning even till noon, saying, 'O Baal, hear us!' But there was no voice; no one answered. Then they leaped about the altar which they had made.

"And so it was, at noon, that Elijah mocked them and said, 'Cry aloud, for he is a god; either he is meditating, or he is busy, or he is on a journey, or perhaps he is sleeping and must be awakened.'

"So they cried aloud, and cut themselves, as was their custom, with knives and lances, until the blood gushed out on them. And when midday was past, they prophesied until the time of the offering of the evening sacrifice. But there was no voice; no one answered, no one paid attention.

"Then Elijah said to all the people, 'Come near to me.' So all the people came near to him. And he repaired the altar of the Lord that was broken down. And Elijah took twelve stones, according to the number of the tribes of the sons of Jacob, to whom the word of the Lord had come, saying, 'Israel shall be your name.'

"Then with the stones he built an altar in the name of the Lord; and he made a trench around the altar large enough to hold two seahs of seed. And he put the wood in order, cut the bull in pieces, and laid it on the wood, and said, 'Fill four water pots with water, and pour it on the burnt sacrifice and on the wood.'

"Then he said, 'Do it a second time,' and they did it a second time; and he said, 'Do it a third time,' and they did it a third time. So the water ran all around the altar; and he also filled the trench with water.

"And it came to pass, at the time of the offering of the evening sacrifice, that Elijah the prophet came near and said, 'Lord God of Abraham, Isaac, and Israel, let it be known this day that You are God in Israel and I am Your servant, and that I have done all these things at Your word. Hear me, O Lord, hear me, that this people may know that You are the Lord God, and that You have turned their hearts back to You again.'

"Then the fire of the Lord fell and consumed the burnt sacrifice, and the wood and the stones and the dust, and it licked up the water that was in the trench. Now when all the people saw it, they fell on their faces; and they said, 'The Lord, He is God! The Lord, He is God!'

"And Elijah said to them, 'Seize the prophets of Baal! Do not let one of them escape!' So they seized them; and Elijah brought them down to the Brook Kishon and executed them there."

Read the passage and meditate on the scriptures. Then pray this prayer: *Father, in the name of Jesus, show me this scene. Show me the frustration of the prophets of Baal as their false god would not—could not answer. Show me Elijah rebuilding the altar of the Lord. Show me the fire coming down from heaven and licking up the water.*

ACTIVATION 69
SEE THE EUNUCHS THROWING JEZEBEL DOWN

In 2 Kings 9:30-35 (KJV), "And when Jehu was come to Jezreel, Jezebel heard of it; and she painted her face, and tired her head, and looked out at a window. And as Jehu entered in at the gate, she said, Had Zimri peace, who slew his master? And he lifted up his face to the window, and said, Who is on my side? who? And there looked out to him two or three eunuchs.

"And he said, Throw her down. So they threw her down: and some of her blood was sprinkled on the wall, and on the horses: and he trode her under foot. And when he was come in, he did eat and drink, and said, Go, see now this cursed woman, and bury her: for she is a king's daughter. And they went to bury her: but they found no more of her than the skull, and the feet, and the palms of her hands."

Pray this prayer: *Father, in the name of Jesus, show me this scene. Show me how Jezebel's face painted and her expression. Show me the conversation between Jezebel and Jehu, then Jehu and the eunuchs. Show me the eunuchs throwing Jezebel down and her remains.*

ACTIVATION 70
SEE THE PARTING OF THE RED SEA

Exodus 14 gives the account of Israelites miraculous exodus. Moses led them out of the Egypt across the Red Sea. In Exodus 14:21-22, we read:

"And Moses stretched out his hand over the sea; and the Lord caused the sea to go back by a strong east wind all that night, and made the sea dry land, and the waters were divided. And the children of Israel went into the midst of the sea upon the dry ground: and the waters were a wall unto them on their right hand, and on their left."

You can read the entire account, where the sea comes back together and drowns in the Egyptian army in the following verses. Pray this prayer:

Father, in the name of Jesus, show me the walls of water that created a pathway for the Israelites. Show me the looks on the faces of both the Israelites and the Egyptians. Show me the walls of water closing back up on the enemy. Put me in awe of Your wonder-working power in this event.

ACTIVATION 71
SEE REVELATION SEALS, TRUMPETS AND BOWLS

In the Book of Revelation, we read about seven seals, seven trumpets and seven bowls. Read the accounts of the seven seals in; the seven trumpets, and the seven bowls. These are dramatic accounts highlighting the ministry of angels in the end times.

SIX SEALS IN REVELATION 6:1-17

Now I saw when the Lamb opened one of the seals; and I heard one of the four living creatures saying with a voice like thunder, "Come and see." And I looked, and behold, a white horse. He who sat on it had a bow; and a crown was given to him, and he went out conquering and to conquer.

When He opened the second seal, I heard the second living creature saying, "Come and see." Another horse, fiery red, went out. And it was granted to the one who sat on it to take peace from the earth, and that people should kill one another; and there was given to him a great sword.

When He opened the third seal, I heard the third living creature say, "Come and see." So I looked, and behold, a black horse, and he who sat on it had a pair of scales in his hand. And I heard a voice in the midst of the four living creatures saying, "A quart of wheat for a denarius, and three quarts of barley for a denarius; and do not harm the oil and the wine."

When He opened the fourth seal, I heard the voice of the fourth living creature saying, "Come and see." So I looked, and behold, a pale horse. And the name of him who sat on it was Death, and Hades followed with him. And power was given to them over a fourth of the earth, to kill with sword, with hunger, with death, and by the beasts of the earth.

When He opened the fifth seal, I saw under the altar the souls of those who had been slain for the word of God and for the testimony which they held. And they cried with a loud voice, saying, "How long, O Lord, holy and true, until You judge and avenge our blood on those who dwell on the earth?" Then a white robe was given to each of them; and it was said to them that they should rest a little while longer, until both the number of their fellow servants and their brethren, who would be killed as they were, was completed.

I looked when He opened the sixth seal, and behold, there was a great earthquake; and the sun became black as sackcloth of hair, and the moon became like blood. And the stars of heaven fell to the earth, as a fig tree drops its late figs when it is shaken by a mighty wind.

Then the sky receded as a scroll when it is rolled up, and every mountain and island was moved out of its place. And the kings of the earth, the great men, the rich men, the commanders, the mighty men, every slave and every free man, hid themselves in the caves and in the rocks of the mountains, and said to the mountains and rocks, "Fall on us and hide us from the face of Him who sits on the throne and from the wrath of the Lamb! For the great day of His wrath has come, and who is able to stand?"

SEVENTH SEAL IN REVELATION 8:1-5

When He opened the seventh seal, there was silence in heaven for about half an hour. And I saw the seven angels who stand before God, and to them were given seven trumpets. Then another angel, having a golden censer, came and stood at the altar. He was given much incense, that he should offer it with the prayers of all the saints upon the golden altar which was before the throne.

And the smoke of the incense, with the prayers of the saints, ascended before God from the angel's hand. Then the angel took the censer, filled it with fire from the altar, and threw it to the earth. And there were noises, thunderings, lightnings, and an earthquake.

THE SEVEN TRUMPETS

The account of the seven trumpets run from Revelation 8 through Revelation 11. Revelation 8:1 begins:

So the seven angels who had the seven trumpets prepared themselves to sound. The first angel sounded: And hail and fire followed, mingled with blood, and they were thrown to the earth. And a third of the trees were burned up, and all green grass was burned up.

Then the second angel sounded: And something like a great mountain burning with fire was thrown into the sea, and a third of the sea became blood. And a third of the living creatures in the sea died, and a third of the ships were destroyed. Then the third angel sounded: And a great star fell from heaven, burning like a torch, and it fell on a third of the rivers and on the springs of water. The name of the star is Wormwood. A third of the waters became wormwood, and many men died from the water, because it was made bitter.

Then the fourth angel sounded: And a third of the sun was struck, a third of the moon, and a third of the stars, so that a third of them were darkened. A third of the day did not shine, and likewise the night. And I looked, and I heard an angel flying through the midst of heaven, saying with a loud voice, "Woe, woe, woe to the inhabitants of the earth, because of the remaining blasts of the trumpet of the three angels who are about to sound!"

Revelation 9 continues: Then the fifth angel sounded: And I saw a star fallen from heaven to the earth. To him was given the key to the bottomless pit. And he opened the bottomless pit, and smoke arose out of the pit like the smoke of a great furnace. So the sun and the air were darkened because of the smoke of the pit.

Then out of the smoke locusts came upon the earth. And to them was given power, as the scorpions of the earth have power. They were commanded not to harm the grass of the earth, or any green thing, or any tree, but only those men who do not have the seal of God on their foreheads. And they were not given authority to kill them, but to torment them for five months. Their torment was like the torment of a scorpion when it strikes a man. In those days men will seek death and will not find it; they will desire to die, and death will flee from them.

The shape of the locusts was like horses prepared for battle. On their heads were crowns of something like gold, and their faces were like the faces of men. They had hair like women's hair, and their teeth were like lions' teeth.

And they had breastplates like breastplates of iron, and the sound of their wings was like the sound of chariots with many horses running into battle. They had tails like scorpions, and there were stings in their tails. Their power was to hurt men five months. And they had as king over them the angel of the bottomless pit, whose name in Hebrew is Abaddon, but in Greek he has the name Apollyon. One woe is past. Behold, still two more woes are coming after these things.

Then the sixth angel sounded: And I heard a voice from the four horns of the golden altar which is before God, saying to the sixth angel who had the trumpet, "Release the four angels who are bound at the great river Euphrates."

So the four angels, who had been prepared for the hour and day and month and year, were released to kill a third of mankind. Now the number of the army of the horsemen was two hundred million; I heard the number of them. And thus I saw the horses in the vision: those who sat on them had breastplates of fiery red, hyacinth blue, and sulfur yellow; and the heads of the horses were like the heads of lions; and out of their mouths came fire, smoke, and brimstone.

By these three plagues a third of mankind was killed—by the fire and the smoke and the brimstone which came out of their mouths. For their power is in their mouth and in their tails;

for their tails are like serpents, having heads; and with them they do harm.

But the rest of mankind, who were not killed by these plagues, did not repent of the works of their hands, that they should not worship demons, and idols of gold, silver, brass, stone, and wood, which can neither see nor hear nor walk. And they did not repent of their murders or their sorceries or their sexual immorality or their thefts.

Revelation 11:15-10 continues, "Then the seventh angel sounded: And there were loud voices in heaven, saying, "The kingdoms of this world have become the kingdoms of our Lord and of His Christ, and He shall reign forever and ever!"

THE SEVEN BOWLS

Revelation 16 offers scenery of the seven bowls of wrath: Then I heard a loud voice from the temple saying to the seven angels, "Go and pour out the bowls of the wrath of God on the earth."

So the first went and poured out his bowl upon the earth, and a foul and loathsome sore came upon the men who had the mark of the beast and those who worshiped his image. Then the second angel poured out his bowl on the sea, and it became blood as of a dead man; and every living creature in the sea died.

Then the third angel poured out his bowl on the rivers and springs of water, and they became blood. And I heard the angel of the waters saying: "You are righteous, O Lord, the One who is and who was and who is to be, because You have judged these things. For they have shed the blood of saints and prophets, and You have given them blood to drink. For it is their just due."

And I heard another from the altar saying, "Even so, Lord God Almighty, true and righteous are Your judgments."

Then the fourth angel poured out his bowl on the sun, and power was given to him to scorch men with fire. And men were scorched with great heat, and they blasphemed the name of God who has power over these plagues; and they did not repent and give Him glory.

Then the fifth angel poured out his bowl on the throne of the beast, and his kingdom became full of darkness; and they gnawed their tongues because of the pain. They blasphemed the God of heaven because of their pains and their sores, and did not repent of their deeds.

Then the sixth angel poured out his bowl on the great river Euphrates, and its water was dried up, so that the way of the kings from the east might be prepared. And I saw three unclean spirits like frogs coming out of the mouth of the dragon, out of the mouth of the beast, and out of the mouth of the false prophet. For they are spirits of demons, performing signs, which go out to the kings of the earth and of the whole world, to gather them to the battle of that great day of God Almighty.

"Behold, I am coming as a thief. Blessed is he who watches, and keeps his garments, lest he walk naked and they see his shame."

And they gathered them together to the place called in Hebrew, Armageddon.

Then the seventh angel poured out his bowl into the air, and a loud voice came out of the temple of heaven, from the throne, saying, "It is done!"

And there were noises and thunderings and lightnings; and there was a great earthquake, such a mighty and great earthquake as had not occurred since men were on the earth.

Now the great city was divided into three parts, and the cities of the nations fell. And great Babylon was remembered before God, to give her the cup of the wine of the fierceness of His wrath. Then every island fled away, and the mountains were not found. And great hail from heaven fell upon men, each hailstone about the weight of a talent. Men blasphemed God because of the plague of the hail, since that plague was exceedingly great.

You may have already started seeing these scenes. After you catch your breath, pray this prayer: *Father, in the name of Jesus, show me the scenes of the seals, trumpets and bowls in order, in real-time. Help me see these events unfold so I can sound the alarm in my generation.*

Pay close attention the actual angels, as well as the finer details in the seals, trumpets and bowls. The seer realm is not void of sound. Be careful to listen to the may sounds that accompany what you see.

ACTIVATION 72
SEE MOSES AND THE BURNING BUSH

Moses had quiet the sight when the Angel of the Lord appeared to him in a flame in a burning bush in Exodus 3:1-6:

Now Moses was tending the flock of Jethro his father-in-law, the priest of Midian. And he led the flock to the back of the desert, and came to Horeb, the mountain of God. And the Angel of the Lord appeared to him in a flame of fire from the midst of a bush. So he looked, and behold, the bush was burning with fire, but the bush was not consumed. Then Moses said, "I will now turn aside and see this great sight, why the bush does not burn."

So when the Lord saw that he turned aside to look, God called to him from the midst of the bush and said, "Moses, Moses!"

And he said, "Here I am."

Then He said, "Do not draw near this place. Take your sandals off your feet, for the place where you stand is holy ground." Moreover He said, "I am the God of your father—the God of Abraham, the God of Isaac, and the God of Jacob." And Moses hid his face, for he was afraid to look upon God.

Notice how Moses turned aside to see the sight. What if Moses didn't have enough spiritual curiosity or was in too big of a hurry to stop and look? Take that as a lesson to be intentional and to look at things that strike your attention.

Pray this prayer: *Father, in the name of Jesus, show me the Angel of the Lord appearing in the flame and the burning bush. Show me the conversation between Moses and the Angel of the Lord. Let me see this awe-inspiring scene.*

Meditate on Exodus 3. What were the weather conditions outside? What did Moses' sandals look like? This must have been a fearful sight as Moses ultimately hid his face.

ACTIVATION 73
SEE THE FALL OF JERICHO

The Lord gave Joshua a strategy to enter the Promised Land. You can read about it in Joshua 6. It was a prophetic act of carrying the ark of the covenant around the city with seven priests bearing seven trumpets. The Lord gave them specific instructions on marching around the city and shouting.

Read the account of the fall of Jericho in Joshua 6:12-20:

And Joshua rose early in the morning, and the priests took up the ark of the Lord. Then seven priests bearing seven trumpets of rams' horns before the ark of the Lord went on continually and blew with the trumpets. And the armed men went before them.

But the rear guard came after the ark of the Lord, while the priests continued blowing the trumpets. And the second day they marched around the city once and returned to the camp. So they did six days.

But it came to pass on the seventh day that they rose early, about the dawning of the day, and marched around the city seven times in the same manner. On that day only they marched around the city seven times. And the seventh time it happened, when the priests blew the trumpets, that Joshua said to the people: "Shout, for the Lord has given you the city!

Now the city shall be doomed by the Lord to destruction, it and all who are in it. Only Rahab the harlot shall live, she and all who are with her in the house, because she hid the messengers that we sent.

And you, by all means abstain from the accursed things, lest you become accursed when you take of the accursed things, and make the camp of Israel a curse, and trouble it. But all the silver and gold, and vessels of bronze and iron, are consecrated to the Lord; they shall come into the treasury of the Lord."

So the people shouted when the priests blew the trumpets. And it happened when the people heard the sound of the trumpet, and the people shouted with a great shout, that the wall fell down flat.

Pray this prayer: *Father, in the name of Jesus, show me this dramatic scene from Scripture. Let me see the priests and the soldiers. Let me hear the trumpet blasts and the shouts. Let me see the walls fall down.*

ACTIVATION 74
SEE ELIJAH TAKEN UP TO HEAVEN IN A CHARIOT

In 2 Kings 2, we read an extraordinary account of Elijah moving out of the earth realm into the spirit realm. 2 Kings 2:9-11 reveals:

"And so it was, when they had crossed over, that Elijah said to Elisha, 'Ask! What may I do for you, before I am taken away from you?'

"Elisha said, 'Please let a double portion of your spirit be upon me.'

"So he said, 'You have asked a hard thing. Nevertheless, if you see me when I am taken from you, it shall be so for you; but if not, it shall not be so.' Then it happened, as they continued on and talked, that suddenly a chariot of fire appeared with horses of fire, and separated the two of them; and Elijah went up by a whirlwind into heaven."

Pray this prayer: *Father, in the name of Jesus, open my eyes and let me see this magnificent site of Elijah's rapture. Let me see the chariot of fire, horses of fire and the whirlwind around Elijah. Let me see the mantle drop and Elisha pick it up.*

Now, meditate on 2 Kings 2:9-11. See the conversation between Elijah and his spiritual son. See the emotions of Elisha as Elijah went on to glory.

ACTIVATION 75
SEE DANIEL IN THE LION'S DEN

Because Daniel would not stop worshipping the Lord or bow down to other gods, he was punished with a sure death sentence. Daniel 6 gives the account of a persecuted prophet being thrown unjustly into the lion's den.

Justice prevailed however, as we see in Daniel 6:22: "My God sent His angel and shut the lions' mouths, so that they have not hurt me, because I was found innocent before Him; and also, O king, I have done no wrong before you."

Pray this prayer: *Father, in the name of Jesus, open my eyes and let me see this perilous scene. Show me the lions. Show me Daniel's faith in action. Let me see the angel that shut the mouth of the lion.*

Meditate on the scene in Daniel 6. What did Daniel do when he faced certain death? Did the lions circle him? Did they fall asleep? How exactly did God shut their mouth? Did the lions struggle?

13

ADVANCED ACTIVATIONS

NOW THAT YOU'VE been through the gateway and intermediate activations, you seer eyes are primed and pumped to go deeper. These advanced activations will take you into deeper dimensions as the Holy Spirit leads. Do not fear but do use wisdom. The deeper you go into the seer dimensions, the more serious the potential error. Over and over again, I will admonish you to check your motives and warn you of witchcraft. Be cautious not to base your theology on dreams, visions and encounters but on the Word of God.

ACTIVATION 76
SEE THE FACE OF GOD

Some in the Bible says the face of God. We know Moses talked to God face to face as a man talked to his friend (see Exodus 33:11). Jacob saw God face to face (see Genesis 32:30). Gideon saw the face of the Angel of the Lord, which is the preincarnate Jesus (see Judges 6:22).

While there is deception in some prophetic circles about seeing the face of God at will, there is biblical precedent for people seeing the face of God. Many people have seen the face of Jesus in dreams and visions.

Pray this prayer: *Father, in the name of Jesus, show me how You are smiling down on me, according to Numbers 6:25-27). Let me see You laughing at Your enemies, according to Psalm 37:1-3. Show me the face of Christ in a dream or vision.*

ACTIVATION 77
SEE INTO WORLD EVENTS

Seeing into world events is generally for the purpose of warning and intercession. This is a higher-level manifestation of the seer anointing. We see Habakkuk invited into this dimension in Habakkuk 1:5, saying to the prophet "Look among the nations and watch—Be utterly astounded! For I will work a work in your days which you would not believe, though it were told you."

If you read Habakkuk 1:14 you see that the Lord's invitation came in response to the prophet's cries in the midst of his prayer burden. Meditate on these verses and pray this prayer:

Father, in the name of Jesus, show me what is going on in nations. Let me see the powers that be plotting against Your will. Show me how the enemy plans to work to turn nation against nation. Let me see which are the goat nations and sheep nations.

Now, cry out to Him as your burden for the nations arises. Ask Him to teach you how to pray.

ACTIVATION 78
SEE THE ROOMS IN HEAVEN

In John 14:2 (CSB), Jesus assured His disciples: "In my Father's house are many rooms; if not, I would have told you."

We know there's a throne room. John saw the throne room in Revelation 4. *Pulpit Commentary* writes: "Heaven is a large place; its possibilities transcend your imagination and exceed your charity."

Many people have seen a war room, libraries, even body parts rooms in heaven. Pray this prayer: *Father, in the name of Jesus, would You show me rooms in heaven? Would You let me see rooms that You created for specific purposes, including prayer, strategy, libraries and the like? Would You show me my room?*

You can start this exercise by seeing the throne room since Revelation 4 gives you a good scriptural account of at least some of what this looks like. As you get comfortable seeing in the throne room, venture out into other rooms in heaven as the Holy Spirit leads you.

ACTIVATION 79
SEEING THE IMAGINATIONS OF MAN'S HEART

The Holy Spirit sees the imaginations of man's heart—and He can allow you to see what's in people's hearts also. We see an example of this in both the Old and New Testaments.

Genesis 6:5 reads, "Then the Lord saw that the wickedness of man was great in the earth, and that every intent of the thoughts of his heart was only evil continually."

And in Matthew 9:3-4 we see Jesus operating in this Holy Spirit gift "Some of the scribes said within themselves, 'This Man blasphemes!' But Jesus, knowing their thoughts, said, 'Why do you think evil in your hearts?'"

Pray this prayer: *Father, in the name of Jesus, show me the imaginations of man's heart. Help me see the motives, reasonings and condition of their heart toward me, someone else or a situation so I can respond rightly and pray accordingly.*

Do this exercise for practical purposes when you are already spiritually sensing something is wrong in a relationship. You can also use this exercise when you have a check in your spirit and need more revelation on if you should align or connect with them further, or if someone is seeking to bring harm to your pastor, and similar situations. Warning: Be careful not to have a manipulative motive or you will end up in witchcraft.

ACTIVATION 80
SEE THE SECRETS OF THE HEART

God can see the secrets of our heart. There are no secrets hidden from His sight. Psalm 44:21 says, "Would not God search this out? For He knows the secrets of the heart."

The Holy Spirit can choose to show us the secrets of someone's heart. This is a function of prophecy highlighted in 1 Corinthians 14:22-25, "But if all prophesy, and an unbeliever or an uninformed person comes in, he is convinced by all, he is convicted by all. And thus the secrets of his heart are revealed; and so, falling down on his face, he will worship God and report that God is truly among you."

Notice the motive is pure. The motive is to convince and convict someone who does not believe. In this case, it's an unbeliever but the Holy Spirit could also open this seer dimension so you can help minister to a believer who is in unbelief. The end of the matter is demonstrating the reality and goodness of God. Any other purpose is witchcraft.

Pray this prayer: *Father, in the name of Jesus, purify my motives. Purify my heart. Show me with secrets of men's hearts, those secret desire and secret needs, so I can minister to them for their edification. Show me secrets of men's hearts so they know Jesus is alive.*

ACTIVATION 81
SEE THE SECRET COUNSEL OF THE WICKED

Demon powers are conspiring against you and others even now. The enemy comes to kill, steal and destroy (see John 10:10). He does this through a network of demon powers who share intelligence they have gathered on you specifically and on mankind in general.

In Psalm 64:2 David writes: "Hide me from the secret plots of the wicked, from the rebellion of the workers of iniquity." We can ask the Holy Spirit to hide us, but we can also ask Him to show us the secret counsel of the wicked spirits against us so we can pray. If we know what the enemy is plotting, we can go on the offense against it or, if the attack is already underway, we can ready an effective defense against it.

Pray this prayer: *Father, in the name of Jesus, show me the counsel of the wicked. Let me see the devices of the enemies and the weapons he is forming against me and those for whom you've called me to intercede. Hide me from the secret plots of the wicked but don't hide the secret plots of the wicked from me.*

ACTIVATION 82
SEE THE KEYS

Scripture has plenty to say about keys. There is the Isaiah 22:22 key: "I will place on his shoulder the key to the house of David; what he opens no one can shut, and what he shuts no one can open."

Jesus spoke of the keys to the kingdom: "I will give you the keys of the kingdom of heaven, and whatever you bind on earth will be bound in heaven, and whatever you loose on earth will be loosed in heaven" (Matthew 16:19).

Jesus also spoke of the keys of death and hades (see Revelation 1:8). John saw an angel with a key to the bottom pit in his hand (see Revelation 20:1).

Having and using the right key at the right time can be critical. When you can't find the key or when you are using the wrong key, you cannot legally gain access to the places God wants to take you.

Pray this prayer: *Father, in the name of Jesus, show me the key of David. Show me the keys the kingdom. Show me the keys of death and hell. Show me the angel with the key to the bottomless pit. Show me the key to the door You are calling me or someone else to walk through next.*

What do the keys look like? How do the keys of the kingdom differ from the keys of death and hell? Are they different colors? Different sizes? What are the various keys of the kingdom, since Jesus mentioned more than one?

ACTIVATION 83
SEE THE NEW HEAVENS AND EARTH

Revelation 21 gives us a picture of the new heavens and new earth. John saw this sight in Revelation 21:1-2: "Then I saw 'a new heaven and a new earth,' for the first heaven and the first earth had passed away, and there was no longer any sea. I saw the Holy City, the new Jerusalem, coming down out of heaven from God, prepared as a bride beautifully dressed for her husband."

Read Revelation 21. John notes the New Jerusalem shone with the glory of God. He describes it as brilliant like a precious jewel and clear as crystal. He called out the gates and the names of the twelve tribes of Israel.

Pray this prayer: *Father, in the name of Jesus, show me these scenes from Revelation 21. Show me what John saw. Show me the gates. Show me the names of the Twelve Apostles of the Lamb on the twelve foundations. Show me what You want me to see.*

ACTIVATION 84
WHAT ELSE DID JESUS DO?

The Bible says, "There are also many other things which Jesus did. Were every one of them to be written, I suppose that not even the world itself could contain the books that would be written. Amen" (John 21:25)

That's an amazing thought. Let it sink in. Not only did Jesus do more than there was room in one book to record. The entire world could not contain record of the miracles, signs, wonders and more Jesus accomplished while walking the earth as fully God, fully man.

Pulpit Commentary writes, "The whole redeeming life, word, and work of the Word made flesh had a quality of infinity about it. The entire evangelic narrative has only touched the fringe of this vast manifestation, a few hours or days of the incomparable life. Every moment of it was infinitely rich in its contents, in its suggestions, in its influence.

"Every act was a revelation of the Father, of the Son, of the Holy Spirit, giving vistas into the eternities, and openings into the heart and bosom of Deity. Let all that thus was done take thought-shape in human minds, and word-shape in human speech, and book-shape or embodiment in human literature, and there are no conceivable limits to its extent."

Pray this prayer: *Father, in the name of Jesus, would You let me see what else Jesus did? Would You show me acts of Christ not recorded in the Bible? Will You show me the miracles, signs and wonders He did that did not fit in the book?*

Now, quiet your heart and wait on the Lord. Only He can show you what else Jesus did. But you can ask and seek.

ACTIVATION 85
SEE INTO CONVERSATIONS

When the king of Syria was warring against Israel, Elisha could see into his room and hear his battle plans. Elisha took what he saw in the spirit to warn the Israelite army so they would have a field advantage.

Eventually the Syrian king was so troubled he thought surely, he had a traitor in his midst. "And one of his servants said, 'None, my lord, O king; but Elisha, the prophet who is in Israel, tells the king of Israel the words that you speak in your bedroom'" (2 Kings 6:12).

Let me make this abundantly clear: We do not have legal permission the spirit to be seeing eavesdroppers and stalkers. Motive matters. God used Elisha to help protect Israel from its enemies. You should not try to see into someone's conversations without an unction from the Holy Spirit. Such a practice is witchcraft. A safer way to do this exercise is to ask the Holy Spirit to show you and let you hear the demons influencing people to do someone harm.

Pray this prayer: *Father, in the name of Jesus, as it serves Your Kingdom purposes, allow me to see into closed-door conversations in hostile governments so I can protect myself and Your people from enemy plots and plans. Show me what demonic forces are orchestrating against Your people so I can stand in the gap, in Jesus' name.*

ACTIVATION 86
SEE THE LOCATION OF PEOPLE & THINGS

The Holy Spirit can show you the location of people. After Elisha gave Naaman a strategy that led to a supernatural healing from leprosy, he offered him a reward. Elisha turned it down and Nathan left. Gehazi, Elisha's servant went after Nathan and accepted the reward under false pretenses. In 2 Kings 5:25-26, we understand Elisha saw where Gehazi was in the spirit.

"Now he went in and stood before his master. Elisha said to him, 'Where did you go, Gehazi?' And he said, 'Your servant did not go anywhere.' Then he said to him, 'Did not my heart go with you when the man turned back from his chariot to meet you? Is it time to receive money and to receive clothing, olive groves and vineyards, sheep and oxen, male and female servants?'"

We have another example: Samuel and Saul's lost donkeys. You can read this account in Samuel 9.

If your motives are pure, you can ask the Holy Spirit to show you in the spirit where someone is. It may be a missing child or someone you are legitimately concerned about and cannot reach by other means. You can practice this by asking the Holy Spirit to show you where someone is, then call them and see if you are accurate. Again, this is not for monitoring and spiritual stalking. Any such practice is blatant witchcraft.

Pray this prayer: *Father, in the name of Jesus, show me the location of someone in the spirit. Let me see where missing children are so I can share it with the authorities. Help me see where lost animals and other objects are so they can be returned to their rightful owner.*

ACTIVATION 87
SEE THE CONDITION OF SOMEONE'S HEART

God sees the condition of our heart. Consider these verses is John 1:47-8 "Jesus saw Nathanael coming toward Him, and said of him, 'Behold, an Israelite indeed, in whom is no deceit!' Nathanael said to Him, 'How do You know me?' Jesus answered and said to him, 'Before Philip called you, when you were under the fig tree, I saw you.'"

Jesus chose His disciples carefully. He would not have called Nathaniel forth if He had seen guile in his heart. Peter rebuked Simon the Sorcerer after seeing the bitter motive in his heart to buy the Holy Ghost: "For I see that you are poisoned by bitterness and bound by iniquity" (Acts 8:23).

The Holy Spirit can allow us to see the condition of someone's heart, either for the sake of avoiding people with toxicity or impure motives toward us or for ministering healing or deliverance to someone's soul. I don't mind repeating myself. Motive matters.

Pray this prayer: *Father, in the name of Jesus, show me the condition of my own heart and lead me into repentance for unknown and presumptuous sins. Show me the condition of hurting hearts so I can minister Your love and compassion to them. Show me those whose hearts are against me or Your purposes so I can stand as a wise gatekeeper in Your kingdom.*

ACTIVATION 88
SEE INTO THE BOOK OF SOMEONE'S LIFE

In Psalm 139:16, David writes, "Your eyes saw my substance, being yet unformed. And in Your book they all were written, the days fashioned for me, when as yet there were none of them." God has the days of everyone's life written in a book.

While ministering to someone, you can ask the Holy Spirit to let you see into the book of their life. This can be especially helpful with inner healing and deliverance ministry, where someone has suppressed memories or trauma.

It can also be helpful in prophesying into someone's future who is hopeless or unsure what next step to take.

The purpose of this is to help people, not to be a spiritual spy for your own enjoyment or to thwart others. Doing so is witchcraft.

Pray this prayer: *Father, in the name of Jesus, would You let me see into the book of people's lives as I minister to them from a heart of love? When You send me into inner healing and deliverance sessions, would You show me what is blocking someone's freedom so they can finally break free? When they are confused about their next steps, will You reveal to me what is written in the book so I can edify, comfort and exhort them?*

ACTIVATION 89
SEE THE SCROLLS

Often the Bible speaks of scrolls. According to *The Seer's Dictionary*, in Bible days, important information, including dictated prophetic words, were found on scrolls. Seers can look into the as the Holy Spirit escorts them.

The Bible speaks of eating scrolls, little scrolls, flying scrolls, and unrolling the scrolls. You can learn more about each in *The Seer's Dictionary*. Jeremiah 36:6 reads: "You go, therefore, and read from the scroll which you have written at my instruction, the words of the Lord, in the hearing of the people in the Lord's house on the day of fasting. And you shall also read them in the hearing of all Judah who come from their cities."

The Dead Sea scrolls were lost, but now they are found. There are other lost scrolls, as well as scrolls mentioned in the Bible we can look into if the Holy Spirit grants us access.

Pray this prayer: *Father, in the name of Jesus, show me what was written on the scroll that was at first sweet in John's mouth but later bitter in his stomach. Show me the content of lost scrolls that contain kingdom mysteries. Let me see the flying scrolls, little scrolls and other scrolls mentioned in Your Word.*

ACTIVATION 90
SEE SCENES FROM HEAVEN

The word heaven appears in the Bible over 300 times. Heaven is God's dwelling place. Since we are citizens of heaven according to Philippians 3:20, we have a legal right to see heaven.

Legally, we are also seated in heavenly places in Christ right now. Christ is sitting at the right hand of the Father. The Holy Spirit has to escort us into these visions. Read Scriptures about heaven. Here are a few to get you started:

"He will swallow up death forever, and the Lord God will wipe away tears from all faces; The rebuke of His people He will take away from all the earth; for the Lord has spoken" (Isaiah 26:18).

"And he showed me a pure river of water of life, clear as crystal, proceeding from the throne of God and of the Lamb. In the middle of its street, and on either side of the river, was the tree of life, which bore twelve fruits, each tree yielding its fruit every month. The leaves of the tree were for the healing of the nations.

"And there shall be no more curse, but the throne of God and of the Lamb shall be in it, and His servants shall serve Him. They shall see His face, and His name shall be on their foreheads. There shall be no night there: They need no lamp nor light of the sun, for the Lord God gives them light. And they shall reign forever and ever" (Revelation 22:1-5).

"And he carried me away in the Spirit to a great and high mountain, and showed me the great city, the holy Jerusalem, descending out of heaven from God, having the glory of God. Her light was like a most precious stone, like a jasper stone, clear as crystal.

"Also she had a great and high wall with twelve gates, and twelve angels at the gates, and names written on them, which are the names of the twelve tribes of the children of Israel: three gates on the east, three gates on the north, three gates on the south, and three gates on the west" (Revelation 21:10-13).

Pray this prayer: *Father, in the name of Jesus, give me glimpses of the river of life. Show me the gates of heaven. Let me see the sea of glass. Allow me to watch as you wipe away tears from the eyes of Your beloved. Show me scenes of heaven as it is, as well as the new heaven and new earth.*

Record what you see.

ACTIVATION 91
SEE THINGS KEPT SECRET SINCE THE FOUNDATION OF THE WORLD

Jesus quote David's Psalm 78:2 when he said, "I will utter things kept secret from the foundation of the world" (Matthew 13:35). Jesus was confirming this reality for New Testament believers. Put your faith on this.

We know God reveals His secrets to His servants the prophets (see Amos 3:7). And Deuteronomy 29:29 assures, "The secret things belong to the Lord our God, but those things which are revealed belong to us and to our children forever, that we may do all the words of this law."

Pray this prayer: *Father, in the name of Jesus, show me things that have been kept secret since the foundation of the world. Let me see the secret things and obtain the revelation that belongs to me as my spiritual birthright. I want to know more about You and how Your kingdom operates.*

Ask with the intention of making intercession when needed, helping people see who God is and who believers are in Christ. Asking with wrong motives will lead you into deception. The enemy will oblige wrong motives.

ACTIVATION 92
SEE THE CHERUBIM

Cherubim are angelic beings (see Exodus 25:20). Cherubim expelled Adam and Eve from the Garden of Eden (see Genesis 3:24). These angelic beings also appear to the right and left of God's throne, and are seen as an image above of the Ark of the Covenant. While seraphim are only mentioned three times in Scripture, cherubim are mentioned 66 times, with the most activity in Exodus and Ezekiel.

Pray this prayer: *Father, in the name of Jesus, let me see the cherubim. Show me the scene where the cherubim expelled Adam and Eve from the Garden of Eden and how they stood guard over* the entryway. Show me the cherubim as they appeared above the Ark of the Covenant and those around God's throne.

Record what you see.

14

EVERY DREAM IN THE BIBLE

THE BIBLE RECORDS 21 dreams. Almost half of those dreams (10) are recorded in the Book of Beginnings, Genesis. Another six are recorded in the Book of Matthew.

Six of the dreamers in the Bible are kings and only one is a woman. It's noteworthy that not all dreamers were serving the Lord.

Read through this list of dreams in the Bible. Pay close attention to the symbols and how God speaks through dreams. If you want more information on how to interpret dreams, pick up my book *Decoding Your Dreams: What God May be Saying to You While You Sleep*.

GOD WARNS ABIMELECH

Genesis 20:3-7, God came to Abimelech in a dream by night, and said to him, "Indeed you are a dead man because of the woman whom you have taken, for she is a man's wife."

But Abimelech had not come near her; and he said, "Lord, will You slay a righteous nation also? Did he not say to me, 'She is my sister'? And she, even she herself said, 'He is my brother.' In the integrity of my heart and innocence of my hands I have done this."

And God said to him in a dream, "Yes, I know that you did this in the integrity of your heart. For I also withheld you from sinning against Me; therefore I did not let you touch her. Now therefore, restore the man's wife; for he is a prophet, and he will pray for you and you shall live. But if you do not restore her, know that you shall surely die, you and all who are yours."

Notice how God spoke to this man directly in a dream. Sometimes God sends angels through dreams or let's events play out for your interpretation.

JACOB SEES ANGELS ASCENDING AND DESCENDING

In Genesis 28:11-13, we read: "So he came to a certain place and stayed there all night, because the sun had set. And he took one of the stones of that place and put it at his head, and he lay down in that place to sleep. Then he dreamed, and behold, a ladder was set up on the earth, and its top reached to heaven; and there the angels of God were ascending and descending on it."

GOD TELLS JACOBI TO GO HOME

Genesis 31:10-13 reads, "And it happened, at the time when the flocks conceived, that I lifted my eyes and saw in a dream, and behold, the rams which leaped upon the flocks were streaked, speckled, and gray-spotted.

"Then the Angel of God spoke to me in a dream, saying, 'Jacob.' And I said, 'Here I am.' And He said, 'Lift your eyes now and see, all the rams which leap on the flocks are streaked, speckled, and gray-spotted; for I have seen all that Laban is doing to you. I am the God of Bethel, where you anointed the pillar and where you made a vow to Me. Now arise, get out of this land, and return to the land of your family.'"

GOD WARNS LABAN

Genesis 31:24 reads, "God had come to Laban the Syrian in a dream by night, and said to him, 'Be careful that you speak to Jacob neither good nor bad.'"

JOSEPH DREAMS OF FAMINE

Genesis 37:5-7 reads, "Now Joseph had a dream, and he told it to his brothers; and they hated him even more. So he said to them, 'Please hear this dream which I have dreamed: There we were, binding sheaves in the field. Then behold, my sheaf arose and also stood upright; and indeed your sheaves stood all around and bowed down to my sheaf.'" This dream is connected with the next dream just a few verses down.

JOSEPH DREAMS ABOUT SUN, MOON AND STARS

Genesis 37:9 reads, "Then he dreamed still another dream and told it to his brothers, and said, "Look, I have dreamed another dream. And this time, the sun, the moon, and the eleven stars bowed down to me."

Notice how the two dreams are related. This is called a recurring dream, according to *The Seer's Dictionary*. When a dream reoccurs, God is working to get your attention.

CUPBEARER DREAMS OF THREE BRANCHES

In Genesis 40:9-11, we read, "Behold, in my dream a vine was before me, and in the vine were three branches; it was as though it budded, its blossoms shot forth, and its clusters brought forth ripe grapes. Then Pharaoh's cup was in my hand; and I took the grapes and pressed them into Pharaoh's cup, and placed the cup in Pharaoh's hand."

BAKER DREAMS OF THREE BASKETS

Genesis 40:16-17 reads, "I also was in my dream, and there were three white baskets on my head.

In the uppermost basket were all kinds of baked goods for Pharaoh, and the birds ate them out of the basket on my head."

PHARAOH DREAMS OF SEVEN FAT COWS

Genesis 41:1-4 reads, "Then it came to pass, at the end of two full years, that Pharaoh had a dream; and behold, he stood by the river. Suddenly there came up out of the river seven cows, fine looking and fat; and they fed in the meadow.

"Then behold, seven other cows came up after them out of the river, ugly and gaunt, and stood by the other cows on the bank of the river. And the ugly and gaunt cows ate up the seven fine looking and fat cows. So Pharaoh awoke."

PHARAOH DREAMS OF SEVEN PLUMB EARS OF GRAIN

Genesis 41:5-7, "He slept and dreamed a second time; and suddenly seven heads of grain came up on one stalk, plump and good. Then behold, seven thin heads, blighted by the east wind, sprang up after them. And the seven thin heads devoured the seven plump and full heads. So Pharaoh awoke, and indeed, it was a dream."

UNNAMED MAN DREAMS OF BREAD ROLLS

In Judges 11:13, we read: "And when Gideon had come, there was a man telling a dream to his companion. He said, 'I have had a dream: To my surprise, a loaf of barley bread tumbled into the camp of Midian; it came to a tent and struck it so that it fell and overturned, and the tent collapsed.'"

SOLOMON DREAMS ABOUT AN INVITATION

In 1 Kings 3:5-15, we read, "At Gibeon the Lord appeared to Solomon in a dream by night; and God said, "Ask! What shall I give you?"

And Solomon said: "You have shown great mercy to Your servant David my father, because he walked before You in truth, in righteousness, and in uprightness of heart with You; You have continued this great kindness for him, and You have given him a son to sit on his throne, as it is this day.

"Now, O Lord my God, You have made Your servant king instead of my father David, but I am a little child; I do not know how to go out or come in. And Your servant is in the midst of Your people whom You have chosen, a great people, too numerous to be numbered or counted.

"Therefore give to Your servant an understanding heart to judge Your people, that I may discern between good and evil. For who is able to judge this great people of Yours?"

"The speech pleased the Lord, that Solomon had asked this thing. Then God said to him: 'Because you have asked this thing, and have not asked long life for yourself, nor have asked riches for yourself, nor have asked the life of your enemies, but have asked for yourself understanding to discern justice, behold, I have done according to your words; see, I have given you a wise and understanding heart, so that there has not been anyone like you before you, nor shall any like you arise after you.

'And I have also given you what you have not asked: both riches and honor, so that there shall not be anyone like you among the kings all your days. So if you walk in My ways, to keep My statutes and My commandments, as your father David walked, then I will lengthen your days.'

"Then Solomon awoke; and indeed, it had been a dream. And he came to Jerusalem and stood before the ark of the covenant of the Lord, offered up burnt offerings, offered peace offerings, and made a feast for all his servants."

NEBUCHADNEZZAR DREAMS OF AN IMAGE

In Daniel 2:31-35, we read, "You, O king, were watching; and behold, a great image! This great image, whose splendor was excellent, stood before you; and its form was awesome.

"This image's head was of fine gold, its chest and arms of silver, its belly and thighs of bronze, its legs of iron, its feet partly of iron and partly of clay. You watched while a stone was cut out without hands, which struck the image on its feet of iron and clay, and broke them in pieces.

"Then the iron, the clay, the bronze, the silver, and the gold were crushed together, and became like chaff from the summer threshing floors; the wind carried them away so that no trace of them was found. And the stone that struck the image became a great mountain and filled the whole earth."

NEBUCHADNEZZAR DREAMS OF HACKED DOWN TREE
In Daniel 4:10-17, we read: "These were the visions of my head while on my bed: I was looking, and behold, a tree in the midst of the earth, and its height was great. The tree grew and became strong; Its height reached to the heavens, and it could be seen to the ends of all the earth.

"Its leaves were lovely, its fruit abundant, and in it was food for all. The beasts of the field found shade under it, the birds of the heavens dwelt in its branches, and all flesh was fed from it.

"I saw in the visions of my head while on my bed, and there was a watcher, a holy one, coming down from heaven. He cried aloud and said thus:

'Chop down the tree and cut off its branches, strip off its leaves and scatter its fruit. Let the beasts get out from under it, and the birds from its branches. Nevertheless leave the stump and roots in the earth, bound with a band of iron and bronze, in the tender grass of the field.

'Let it be wet with the dew of heaven, and let him graze with the beasts on the grass of the earth. Let his heart be changed from that of a man, let him be given the heart of a beast, and let seven times pass over him.

'This decision is by the decree of the watchers, and the sentence by the word of the holy ones, in order that the living may know that the Most High rules in the kingdom of men gives it to whomever He will, and sets over it the lowest of men.'"

DANIEL DREAMS OF FOUR BEASTS

Daniel 7:1-8 records Daniel's dream of the four beasts:

"In the first year of Belshazzar king of Babylon, Daniel had a dream and visions of his head while on his bed. Then he wrote down the dream, telling the main facts.

"Daniel spoke, saying, 'I saw in my vision by night, and behold, the four winds of heaven were stirring up the Great Sea. And four great beasts came up from the sea, each different from the other.

'The first was like a lion, and had eagle's wings. I watched till its wings were plucked off; and it was lifted up from the earth and made to stand on two feet like a man, and a man's heart was given to it.

'And suddenly another beast, a second, like a bear. It was raised up on one side, and had three ribs in its mouth between its teeth. And they said thus to it: 'Arise, devour much flesh!'

'After this I looked, and there was another, like a leopard, which had on its back four wings of a bird. The beast also had four heads, and dominion was given to it.

'After this I saw in the night visions, and behold, a fourth beast, dreadful and terrible, exceedingly strong. It had huge iron teeth; it was devouring, breaking in pieces, and trampling the residue with its feet. It was different from all the beasts that were before it, and it had ten horns.

'I was considering the horns, and there was another horn, a little one, coming up among them, before whom three of the first horns were plucked out by the roots. And there, in this horn, were eyes like the eyes of a man, and a mouth speaking pompous words.'"

JOSEPH DREAMS ABOUT HIS FIANCÉ

Matthew 1:18-24 records the dream Joseph had concerning Mary, the mother of Jesus, after she told him she was pregnant:

Now the birth of Jesus Christ was as follows: After His mother Mary was betrothed to Joseph, before they came together, she was found with child of the Holy Spirit. Then Joseph her husband, being a just man, and not wanting to make her a public example, was minded to put her away secretly.

But while he thought about these things, behold, an angel of the Lord appeared to him in a dream, saying, "Joseph, son of David, do not be afraid to take to you Mary your wife, for that which is conceived in her is of the Holy Spirit. And she will bring forth a Son, and you shall call His name Jesus, for He will save His people from their sins."

So all this was done that it might be fulfilled which was spoken by the Lord through the prophet, saying: "Behold, the virgin shall be with child, and bear a Son, and they shall call His name Immanuel," which is translated, "God with us."

Then Joseph, being aroused from sleep, did as the angel of the Lord commanded him and took to him his wife.

MAGI RECEIVES A WARNING DREAM

Matthew 2:12 records the account of the Magi's dream after visiting the baby Jesus and presenting Him with gifts: "Then, being divinely warned in a dream that they should not return to Herod, they departed for their own country another way."

JOSEPH DREAMS ABOUT GOING TO EGYPT

Matthew 2:13-14 records the account of Joseph's dream about protecting Jesus: Now when they had departed, behold, an angel of the Lord appeared to Joseph in a dream, saying, "Arise, take the young Child and His mother, flee to Egypt, and stay there until I bring you word; for Herod will seek the young Child to destroy Him.

"When he arose, he took the young Child and His mother by night and departed for Egypt, and was there until the death of Herod, that it might be fulfilled which was spoken by the Lord through the prophet, saying, "Out of Egypt I called My Son."

JOSEPH DREAMS ABOUT RETURNING TO ISRAEL

Matthew 2:19-21 records the account of Joseph's dream about returning with Jesus to Israel: Now when Herod was dead, behold, an angel of the Lord appeared in a dream to Joseph in Egypt, saying, "Arise, take the young Child and His mother, and go to the land of Israel, for those who sought the young Child's life are dead." Then he arose, took the young Child and His mother, and came into the land of Israel.

JOSEPH DREAMS ABOUT AVOIDING JUDEA

Matthew 2:22-23 records Joseph's dream with a warning to avoid Judea: "But when he heard that Archelaus was reigning over Judea instead of his father Herod, he was afraid to go there. And being warned by God in a dream, he turned aside into the region of Galilee. And he came and dwelt in a city called Nazareth, that it might be fulfilled which was spoken by the prophets, "He shall be called a Nazarene."

PONTIUS PILATE'S WIFE DREAMS ABOUT JESUS

Matthew 27:19 reads, "When he was set down on the judgment seat, his wife sent unto him, saying, Have thou nothing to do with that just man: for I have suffered many things this day in a dream because of him." We don't know all the details of her dream, but we know it convinced her that Jesus was telling the truth.

15

SEE VISIONS FROM THE BIBLE

THE HOLY SPIRIT CAN Show you visions from the Bible. There are far more visions than dreams recorded in the Bible, which could signal God speaks to us more while we are awake than when we are asleep. Every vision in the Bible is listed later in this book, so you can continue practicing. But here are a few great visions you can press into now. Keep in mind you cannot create doctrines based off seer revelations.

ACTIVATION 93
SEE VISIONS THAT DEAL WITH THE END-TIMES

Among others, Daniel and John the Revelator, had visions of the end-times. With regard to what he saw in the spirit, an angel told Daniel, "Understand, son of man, that the vision refers to the time of the end" (Daniel 8:17).

Study what the Bible tells us about the end times so you are grounded in the Word of God. Some Scriptures to consider include:

Joel 8:28-32, "And it shall come to pass afterward that I will pour out My Spirit on all flesh; Your sons and your daughters shall prophesy, your old men shall dream dreams, your young men shall see visions, and also on My menservants and on My maidservants I will pour out My Spirit in those days.

"And I will show wonders in the heavens and in the earth: blood and fire and pillars of smoke. The sun shall be turned into darkness, and the moon into blood, before the coming of the great and awesome day of the Lord.

"And it shall come to pass that whoever calls on the name of the Lord shall be saved. For in Mount Zion and in Jerusalem there shall be deliverance, as the Lord has said, among the remnant whom the Lord calls."

2 Peter 3:10-13, "But the day of the Lord will come as a thief in the night, in which the heavens will pass away with a great noise, and the elements will melt with fervent heat; both the earth and the works that are in it will be burned up.

"Therefore, since all these things will be dissolved, what manner of persons ought you to be in holy conduct and godliness, looking for and hastening the coming of the day of God, because of which the heavens will be dissolved, being on fire, and the elements will melt with fervent heat? Nevertheless we, according to His promise, look for new heavens and a new earth in which righteousness dwells."

Zechariah 14:1-5, "Behold, the day of the Lord is coming, and your spoil will be divided in your midst. For I will gather all the nations to battle against Jerusalem; The city shall be taken, the houses rifled, and the women ravished. Half of the city shall go into captivity, but the remnant of the people shall not be cut off from the city.

"Then the Lord will go forth and fight against those nations, as He fights in the day of battle. And in that day His feet will stand on the Mount of Olives, which faces Jerusalem on the east.

"And the Mount of Olives shall be split in two, from east to west, making a very large valley; Half of the mountain shall move toward the north and half of it toward the south. Then you shall flee through My mountain valley, for the mountain valley shall reach to Azal. Yes, you shall flee as you fled from the earthquake in the days of Uzziah king of Judah. Thus the Lord my God will come, and all the saints with You."

Zechariah 14:8-9, "And in that day it shall be that living waters shall flow from Jerusalem, half of them toward the eastern sea and half of them toward the western sea; In both summer and winter it shall occur. And the Lord shall be King over all the earth. In that day it shall be—"The Lord is one," And His name one."

Read the end-times visions in the Bible and what Jesus said about the end-times. The Book of Revelation offers chapter after chapter of vivid accounts and encounters. Pray this prayer:

Father, in the name of Jesus, give me visions that deal with the end-times. Let me see the Battle at Armageddon. Let me see what John and Daniel and other prophets in Your Word saw. Prepare me for the final battle by showing me what I need to see for myself and to warn others.

Have faith to see. God is actively releasing such dreams and visions to many across the Body of Christ to those who will make intercession.

ACTIVATION 94
SEE EZEKIEL'S VISION OF LIVING CREATURES AND WHEEL WITHIN A WHEEL

Ezekiel 1 outlines a dramatic vision that should cause you to hunger to go deeper in the seer dimensions. Ezekiel saw a whirlwind come out of the north, brightness and fire. He saw four living creatures, each one with four faces. He saw a wheel within a wheel. This vision is full of vivid scenes and symbols that are difficult for the mind to understand. Let's read the vision:

"Now it came to pass in the thirtieth year, in the fourth month, on the fifth day of the month, as I was among the captives by the River Chebar, that the heavens were opened and I saw visions of God. On the fifth day of the month, which was in the fifth year of King Jehoiachin's captivity, the word of the Lord came expressly to Ezekiel the priest, the son of Buzi, in the land of the Chaldeans by the River Chebar; and the hand of the Lord was upon him there.

"Then I looked, and behold, a whirlwind was coming out of the north, a great cloud with raging fire engulfing itself; and brightness was all around it and radiating out of its midst like the color of amber, out of the midst of the fire. Also from within it came the likeness of four living creatures. And this was their appearance: they had the likeness of a man.

"Each one had four faces, and each one had four wings. Their legs were straight, and the soles of their feet were like the soles of calves' feet. They sparkled like the color of burnished bronze. The hands of a man were under their wings on their four sides; and each of the four had faces and wings. Their wings touched one another. The creatures did not turn when they went, but each one went straight forward.

"As for the likeness of their faces, each had the face of a man; each of the four had the face of a lion on the right side, each of the four had the face of an ox on the left side, and each of the four had the face of an eagle. Thus were their faces. Their wings stretched upward; two wings of each one touched one another, and two covered their bodies. And each one went straight forward; they went wherever the spirit wanted to go, and they did not turn when they went.

"As for the likeness of the living creatures, their appearance was like burning coals of fire, like the appearance of torches going back and forth among the living creatures. The fire was bright, and out of the fire went lightning. And the living creatures ran back and forth, in appearance like a flash of lightning.

"Now as I looked at the living creatures, behold, a wheel was on the earth beside each living creature with its four faces. The appearance of the wheels and their workings was like the color of beryl, and all four had the same likeness. The appearance of their workings was, as it were, a wheel in the middle of a wheel.

"When they moved, they went toward any one of four directions; they did not turn aside when they went. As for their rims, they were so high they were awesome; and their rims were full of eyes, all around the four of them. When the living creatures went, the wheels went beside them; and when the living creatures were lifted up from the earth, the wheels were lifted up.

"Wherever the spirit wanted to go, they went, because there the spirit went; and the wheels were lifted together with them, for the spirit of the living creatures was in the wheels. When those went, these went; when those stood, these stood; and when those were lifted up from the earth, the wheels were lifted up together with them, for the spirit of the living creatures was in the wheels.

"The likeness of the firmament above the heads of the living creatures was like the color of an awesome crystal, stretched out over their heads. And under the firmament their wings spread out straight, one toward another. Each one had two which covered one side, and each one had two which covered the other side of the body.

"When they went, I heard the noise of their wings, like the noise of many waters, like the voice of the Almighty, a tumult like the noise of an army; and when they stood still, they let down their wings. A voice came from above the firmament that was over their heads; whenever they stood, they let down their wings.

"And above the firmament over their heads was the likeness of a throne, in appearance like a sapphire stone; on the likeness of the throne was a likeness with the appearance of a man high above it.

"Also from the appearance of His waist and upward I saw, as it were, the color of amber with the appearance of fire all around within it; and from the appearance of His waist and downward I saw, as it were, the appearance of fire with brightness all around. Like the appearance of a rainbow in a cloud on a rainy day, so was the appearance of the brightness all around it. This was the appearance of the likeness of the glory of the Lord."

Meditate on Ezekiel 1. Read it over and over in different translations of the Bible. Pray this prayer: *Father, in the name of Jesus, would You let me see exactly what Ezekiel saw in the vision, and even more? Let me see the brilliance of the sapphire stones. Let me hear the noise of many waters.* Record what you see.

ACTIVATION 95
SEE EZEKIEL'S VISION OF VALLEY OF THE DRY BONES

Ezekiel 37:1-14 contains a vision of the valley of dry bones. This passage has been a popular sermon topic for decades. Let's read it through:

The hand of the Lord came upon me and brought me out in the Spirit of the Lord, and set me down in the midst of the valley; and it was full of bones. Then He caused me to pass by them all around, and behold, there were very many in the open valley; and indeed they were very dry. And He said to me, "Son of man, can these bones live?"

So I answered, "O Lord God, You know."

Again, He said to me, "Prophesy to these bones, and say to them, 'O dry bones, hear the word of the Lord! Thus says the Lord God to these bones: "Surely I will cause breath to enter into you, and you shall live. I will put sinews on you and bring flesh upon you, cover you with skin and put breath in you; and you shall live. Then you shall know that I am the Lord."

So I prophesied as I was commanded; and as I prophesied, there was a noise, and suddenly a rattling; and the bones came together, bone to bone. Indeed, as I looked, the sinews and the flesh came upon them, and the skin covered them over; but there was no breath in them.

Also He said to me, "Prophesy to the breath, prophesy, son of man, and say to the breath, 'Thus says the Lord God: "Come from the four winds, O breath, and breathe on these slain, that they may live." So I prophesied as He commanded me, and breath came into them, and they lived, and stood upon their feet, an exceedingly great army.

Then He said to me, "Son of man, these bones are the whole house of Israel. They indeed say, 'Our bones are dry, our hope is lost, and we ourselves are cut off!' Therefore prophesy and say to them, 'Thus says the Lord God: "Behold, O My people, I will open your graves and cause you to come up from your graves, and bring you into the land of Israel. Then you shall know that I am the Lord, when I have opened your graves, O My people, and brought you up from your graves. I will put My Spirit in you, and you shall live, and I will place you in your own land. Then you shall know that I, the Lord, have spoken it and performed it," says the Lord.'"

Notice in verse one how the hand of the Lord came upon him and brought him out in the spirit and set him down in the midst of the valley. Notice also how he interacted within the vision by prophesying out of what he saw.

Read and meditate on this vision. Pray this payer: *Father, in the name of Jesus, would You take me up in the spirit and set me down in the Valley of Dry Bones? Would You let me experience what Ezekiel saw?*

What do you see? Focus on the bones coming back together. Ask the Holy Spirit to prophesy through you to the dry bones in your life, city or nation. Record what you see and say.

ACTIVATION 96
SEE ISAIAH'S VISION OF GOD

In Isaiah 6:1-8, as part of his calling, Isaiah saw the Lord sitting on a throne, high and lifted up. His train filled the temple. He also saw seraphim with six wings. He heard the sounds of the seraphim crying aloud. He saw the posts of the door shaking and the house filled with smoke.

Read Isaiah 6:1-8 over and over again:

In the year that King Uzziah died, I saw the Lord sitting on a throne, high and lifted up, and the train of His robe filled the temple. Above it stood seraphim; each one had six wings: with two he covered his face, with two he covered his feet, and with two he flew. And one cried to another and said:

"Holy, holy, holy is the Lord of hosts; The whole earth is full of His glory!"

And the posts of the door were shaken by the voice of him who cried out, and the house was filled with smoke. So I said:

Woe is me, for I am undone! Because I am a man of unclean lips, and I dwell in the midst of a people of unclean lips; For my eyes have seen the King, The Lord of hosts.

Then one of the seraphim flew to me, having in his hand a live coal which he had taken with the tongs from the altar. And he touched my mouth with it, and said:

"Behold, this has touched your lips; Your iniquity is taken away, and your sin purged."

Also I heard the voice of the Lord, saying: "Whom shall I send, and who will go for Us?" Then I said, "Here am I! Send me."

Notice the results of this encounter, namely Isaiah's fear of the Lord. Some seers and seeing people emerge from encounters without any fear or the Lord. This is unnatural. Anyone who encountered the Lord in Scripture walked away with an awe and usually in fear and trembling.

Meditate one each word of this vision. Pray this prayer:

Father, in the name of Jesus, let me see what Isaiah saw and feel what Isaiah felt in this vision. Send an angel to put a coal to my mouth to cleanse my lips. I am committed to Your service. I commit my eyes to You, my ears to You, and my heart to You. Take my eyes and use them for Your glory.

ACTIVATION 97
SEE DANIELS VISION OF THE ANCIENT OF DAYS

In Daniel 7:9-10, we see the prophet had a vision of the Ancient of Days, another name for God. Read the account:

"I watched till thrones were put in place, and the Ancient of Days was seated; His garment was white as snow, and the hair of His head was like pure wool. His throne was a fiery flame, its wheels a burning fire;

"A fiery stream issued and came forth from before Him. A thousand thousands ministered to Him; Ten thousand times ten thousand stood before Him. The court was seated, and the books were opened."

Notice how Daniel watched. Daniel had a tenacity to look and keep on looking and to watch and keep on watching. Daniel described the Lord in fine detail, as one who saw him face to face. Although his words could not fully explain what he saw, he used the best vocabulary he had.

Again, in Daniel 7:13-14, the prophet continues:

"I was watching in the night visions, and behold, One like the Son of Man, Coming with the clouds of heaven! He came to the Ancient of Days and they brought Him near before Him.

"Then to Him was given dominion and glory and a kingdom, that all peoples, nations, and languages should serve Him. His dominion is an everlasting dominion, which shall not pass away, and His kingdom the one which shall not be destroyed."

Notice how Daniel also say Jesus coming with the clouds in heaven and interact with the Ancient of Days. What a sight to see two members of the Godhead in this manner!

Finally in Daniel 7:21-22 we read: "I was watching; and the same horn was making war against the saints, and prevailing against them, until the Ancient of Days came, and a judgment was made in favor of the saints of the Most High, and the time came for the saints to possess the kingdom."

Prayer this prayer, then meditate on the vision:

Father, in the name of Jesus, will You show me Daniel's vision of the Ancient of Days? Will You open my eyes so I can see Your white-as-snow garments, hair like pure wool, along with the fiery flaming throne? Will You let me watch the thousands of angels ministering to You, and see into the open books?

What language would you use to describe that scene? Record what you see.

ACTIVATION 98
SEE THE TRANSFIGURATION OF JESUS

In Matthew 17:1-9, the Bible records one of the most dramatic and controversial events in Scripture: the transfiguration of Jesus with the appearance of Moses and Elijah. Read the account for yourself:

Now after six days Jesus took Peter, James, and John his brother, led them up on a high mountain by themselves; and He was transfigured before them. His face shone like the sun, and His clothes became as white as the light.

And behold, Moses and Elijah appeared to them, talking with Him. Then Peter answered and said to Jesus, "Lord, it is good for us to be here; if You wish, let us make here three tabernacles: one for You, one for Moses, and one for Elijah."

While he was still speaking, behold, a bright cloud overshadowed them; and suddenly a voice came out of the cloud, saying, "This is My beloved Son, in whom I am well pleased. Hear Him!" And when the disciples heard it, they fell on their faces and were greatly afraid. But Jesus came and touched them and said, "Arise, and do not be afraid." When they had lifted up their eyes, they saw no one but Jesus only.

Now as they came down from the mountain, Jesus commanded them, saying, "Tell the vision to no one until the Son of Man is risen from the dead."

Notice how Jesus told them not to tell the vision. There are times when the Holy Spirit will allow you to see something and instruct you not to share it. Obey Him.

Notice the rich descriptions about Jesus: His face shone like the sun. That means it was probably so bright it was blinding. His clothes became as white as the light. This is dramatic language that probably doesn't do the encounter justice, as words fail in times like that. Pray this prayer:

Father, in the name of Jesus, would You let you see what Peter, James and John saw at the Mount of Transfiguration? Will You show me the face of Christ shining like the sun, His clothes white as light, and Moses and Elijah speaking with Him? Will You let me hear the conversation and the voice of God thundering to the disciples.

If and when the Holy Spirit shows you this scene, it may overwhelm you. Keep on looking. Notice how Peter was so overcome and disoriented by the vison he wanted to build tabernacles for Jesus, Moses and Elijah. Listen closely. Can you hear what these three were talking about? Why did God arrange this meeting between the three of them? Record what you see in a journal.

ACTIVATION 99
SEE ZECHARIAH'S VISION OF THE HORSEMEN

In Zechariah 1:7-11 and Zechariah 6:1-8, we see one of the prophet's night visions. This is also an apocalyptic vision. According to *The Seer's Dictionary*, apocalyptic means, "of, relating to, or resembling an apocalypse; apocalyptic events; forecasting the ultimate destiny of the world." Zechariah saw the four horsemen of the apocalypse.

Zechariah 1:7-11 reads: On the twenty-fourth day of the eleventh month, which is the month Shebat, in the second year of Darius, the word of the Lord came to Zechariah the son of Berechiah, the son of Iddo the prophet: I saw by night, and behold, a man riding on a red horse, and it stood among the myrtle trees in the hollow; and behind him were horses: red, sorrel, and white.

Then I said, "My lord, what are these?" So the angel who talked with me said to me, "I will show you what they are." And the man who stood among the myrtle trees answered and said, "These are the ones whom the Lord has sent to walk to and fro throughout the earth."

So they answered the Angel of the Lord, who stood among the myrtle trees, and said, "We have walked to and fro throughout the earth, and behold, all the earth is resting quietly."

Notice how this was a night vision. Zechariah had a series of profound night visions. A night vision is a vision you have a night, often during the moments between sleeping and becoming fully awake, according to The Seer's Dictionary.

Zechariah 6:1-8 reads: "Then I turned and raised my eyes and looked, and behold, four chariots were coming from between two mountains, and the mountains were mountains of bronze. With the first chariot were red horses, with the second chariot black horses, with the third chariot white horses, and with the fourth chariot dappled horses—strong steeds. Then I answered and said to the angel who talked with me, "What are these, my lord?"

And the angel answered and said to me, "These are four spirits of heaven, who go out from their station before the Lord of all the earth. The one with the black horses is going to the north country, the white are going after them, and the dappled are going toward the south country." Then the strong steeds went out, eager to go, that they might walk to and fro throughout the earth.

And He said, "Go, walk to and fro throughout the earth." So they walked to and fro throughout the earth. And He called to me, and spoke to me, saying, "See, those who go toward the north country have given rest to My Spirit in the north country."

Meditate on Zechariah's night visions. Notice the similarities between Zechariah's night visions and John the Revelator's ecstatic experience. Notice the differences. Pray this prayer:

Father, in the name of Jesus, show me each of the four horses in splendid color. Send the angel that spoke to Zechariah to speak to me about what I am seeing.

ACTIVATION 100
SEE ZECHARIAH'S VISION OF THE LAMPSTAND AND OLIVE TREES

Zechariah 4 reveals a vision of the lampstand and olive trees. Consider the vision, then answer the questions at the bottom of this activation:

Now the angel who talked with me came back and wakened me, as a man who is wakened out of his sleep. And he said to me, "What do you see?"

So I said, "I am looking, and there is a lampstand of solid gold with a bowl on top of it, and on the stand seven lamps with seven pipes to the seven lamps. Two olive trees are by it, one at the right of the bowl and the other at its left." So I answered and spoke to the angel who talked with me, saying, "What are these, my lord?"

Then the angel who talked with me answered and said to me, "Do you not know what these are?"

And I said, "No, my lord." So he answered and said to me: "This is the word of the Lord to Zerubbabel: 'Not by might nor by power, but by My Spirit,' says the Lord of hosts. 'Who are you, O great mountain? Before Zerubbabel you shall become a plain!

And he shall bring forth the capstone with shouts of "Grace, grace to it!"

Moreover the word of the Lord came to me, saying: "The hands of Zerubbabel have laid the foundation of this temple; His hands shall also finish it. Then you will know that the Lord of hosts has sent Me to you. For who has despised the day of small things? For these seven rejoice to see the plumb line in the hand of Zerubbabel.

They are the eyes of the Lord, which scan to and fro throughout the whole earth.

Then I answered and said to him, "What are these two olive trees—at the right of the lampstand and at its left?" And I further answered and said to him, "What are these two olive branches that drip into the receptacles of the two gold pipes from which the golden oil drains?"

Then he answered me and said, "Do you not know what these are?"

And I said, "No, my lord."

So he said, "These are the two anointed ones, who stand beside the Lord of the whole earth."

Notice in verse one how the prophet is looking. When God shows you something, you have to look with full attention to capture the visual detail with accuracy.

Notice the use of repetitive numbers in the vision, specifically the number seven. Seven is a number of perfection. When you see numbers in a vision, pay attention. When they are repetitive, understand the Holy Spirit is emphasizing a point. Search it out.

Notice also how Zechariah, like John and Daniel, speaks to an angel for explanation. This is not unusual. If you are confounded by the vision, look for the angel of explanation close by. Cry out for understanding.

Meditate on Zechariah 4. Ask the Holy Spirit to let you see what Zechariah saw. Count the numbers lamps and the pipes to the lamps as a practice for noticing patterns and numbers in future visions. Look around for the angel of explanation in this and other visions. Pray this prayer, then read the vision and see it:

Father, in the name of Jesus, help me see what Zechariah saw in all its vivid glory. Help me not to turn my head away until I notice the finer details of this vision. Help me understand the deeper messages. Release angels of explanation to teach me what Your Spirit is showing me.

Record what you see in a journal.

ACTIVATION 101
SEE ZECHARIAH'S VISION OF HORNS & CRAFTSMEN

Zechariah 1:18-21 reads, "Then I raised my eyes and looked, and there were four horns. And I said to the angel who talked with me, 'What are these?' So he answered me, 'These are the horns that have scattered Judah, Israel, and Jerusalem.' Then the Lord showed me four craftsmen. And I said, 'What are these coming to do?'

"So he said, 'These are the horns that scattered Judah, so that no one could lift up his head; but the craftsmen are coming to terrify them, to cast out the horns of the nations that lifted up their horn against the land of Judah to scatter it.'"

Notice how Zechariah raised his eyes to look. He was alert in the spirit. Notice again how he was talking with an angel, not merely having a chat but for the sake of interpreting revelation.

Ask the Holy Spirit to show you the same vision Zechariah saw, with the four horns and the four craftsmen. As you begin to see things you don't understand, ask the Holy Spirit to show you what it means. Pray this prayer, then read the vision and see it:

Father, in the name of Jesus, let me see Zechariah's vision of the horns and craftsman. Help me to stay alert in the spirit at all times. Help me not rely on what I think I know about this verse but be open to going deeper into the truth revealed in this vision.

Record what you see in a journal.

16

ALL THE VISIONS IN THE BIBLE

IN NUMBERS 12:6, GOD SAYS, "Hear now My words: if there is a prophet among you, I, the Lord, make Myself known to him in a vision; I speak to him in a dream." Here is a list of all the visions in the Bible. You can refer to them to do additional seer activations.

Genesis 15:1-17 records Abraham's vision concerning his descendants.

Genesis 28:12 records Jacob's vision of a ladder with angels ascending and descending.

Genesis 46:2 records Jacob's visions of the night.

Exodus 3:2 records Moses' encounter with the Angel of the Lord in the burning bush.

Exodus 24:9-11 records when Moses and elders from Israel saw God.

Exodus 24:17 records a vision of God's glory on top of a mountain.

Exodus 33:18-33 records an encounter in which Moses saw God's glory.

Joshua 5:13-15 records Joshua's encounter with the Captain of the Hosts.

1 Samuel 3:11-15 records Samuel's encounter with the Lord where he received a word of judgment against the house of Eli.

1 Kings 22:17 records Michaiah's vision of an Israelite defeat.

1 Kings 22:19 records Michaiah's vision of the Lord sitting on the throne with His angels.

2 Kings 6:17 records the Elisah's servant's vision of the chariots of fire.

1 Chronicles 21:15-18 records David's vision of destroyer angels with a drawn sword stretched out over Jerusalem.

Job 4:12-16 records Eliphaz's vision of the Spirit of God that caused him tremble in fear and his bones shake.

Isaiah 1 records the call of Isaiah, his vision of God and an angel with a burning coal of fire.

Isaiah 6:1-13 records Isaiah's vision of the God in His glorious temple.

Isaiah 21:1-3 records Isaiah's distressing vision of treacherous dealers.

Isaiah 2 records Isaiah's troubling vision of the Valley of Vision.

Jeremiah 1:11 records Jeremiah's vision of the almond three.

Jeremiah 1:13 records Jeremiah's vision of the boiling pot.

Ezekiel 1:4 records Ezekiel's vision of the glory of God.

Ezekiel 1:5-25 records Ezekiel's vision of the four living creatures.

Ezekiel 1:26-28 records Ezekiel's vision of God and His throne.

Ezekiel 2:9 records Ezekiel's vision of a scroll.

Ezekiel 10:1-7 records Ezekiel's vision of the glory of the Lord departing from the temple.

Ezekiel 37:1-4 records Ezekiel's vision of the Valley of the Dry Bones.

Ezekiel 40 records Ezekiel's vision of a new city and a new temple.

Ezekiel 43:10 records Ezekiel's vision of the temple, God's dwelling place.

Ezekiel 47:1-12 records Ezekiel's vision of the healing waters and trees.

Daniel 7:9-27 records Daniel's vision of the Ancient of Days.

Daniel 8 records Daniel's vision of the ram and the goat.

Daniel 10 records Daniel's vision of an angel that brought him a prayer answer.

Amos 7:1-3 records Amos' vision of the locusts swarming.

Amos 7:4-6 records Amos' vision of God calling for conflict by fire.

Amos 7:7-9 records Amos' vision of the man with the plumb line.

Amos 8:1-2 records Amos' vision of a basket of summer fruit.

Amos 9:1 records Amos' vision of the Lord standing on the altar releasing instructions.

Zechariah 1:8-11 records Zechariah's vision of a man riding a red horse.

Zechariah 1:18-21 records Zechariah's vision of the four horns.

Zechariah 3:1-5 records Zechariah's vision of Joshua the high priest in filthy rags.

Zechariah 4:1-14 records Zechariah's vision of the golden candlestick.

Zechariah 5:1-14 records Zechariah's vision of the flying scroll.

Zechariah 6:1-8 records Zechariah's vision of chariots and mountains.

Luke 1:13-22 records Zacharias' vision of an angel confirming his wife's pregnancy.

Matthew 3:16 records John the Baptist's vision of the Holy Spirit descending on Jesus like a dove. This is also recorded in Mark 1:10, Luke 3:22 and John 1:32-34.

Matthew 17:19 records the vision Peter, James and John saw of Jesus transfigured, talking with Moses and Elijah. This is also recorded in Luke 9:28-36.

Acts 2:2-3 records the Upper Room disciples' vision of tongues like cloven fire falling upon them during the Baptism of the Holy Spirit on Pentecost.

Acts 2:7:55-56 records Stephen's vision of Jesus sitting at the right hand of the Father in heaven.

Acts 9:3-6 records Paul's vision of Jesus on the road to Damascus.

Acts 9:10-11 records Ananias' vision of the Lord giving him instructions to find Paul and pray for him.

Acts 9:12 records Paul's vision of Ananias coming to lay his hands on him to restore his sight.

Acts 10:4 records the centurion Cornelius' vison of an angel telling him to call for Peter.

Acts 10:9-18 records Peter's trance in which he saw a vision of unclean animals coming down on a sheet.

Acts 18:9-10 records Paul's vision of the Lord telling him not to be afraid of preaching in Corinth.

Acts 22:17:21 records Paul's vision during a trance in which Paul saw Jesus telling him to get out of Jerusalem quickly.

2 Corinthians 12:1-6 record's Paul's vision of Paradise.

Revelation 1:10-20 records John's vision of the golden candlesticks.

Revelation 4:1 records John's vision of a door standing open in heaven.

Revelation 4:2-11 records John's vision of the throne in heaven encircled by a rainbow, with 24 thrones, 24 elders, the sea of glass and four living creatures.

Revelation 5:1-5 records John's vision of the seven seals.

Revelation 5:8 records John's visions of the four beasts and 24 elders with golden vials containing the prayers of the saints.

Revelation 6 records John's vision of six seals being opened, including four horses, celestial events, and a quaking earth.

Revelation 7:1-8 records John's vision of the seventh seal being opened and the sealing of the 144,000.

Revelation 7:9-16 records John's vision of the multitudes who came out of the great tribulation.

Revelation 8:1-6 records John's vision of what happened when the seventh seal was opened, how it was silent in heaven for one hour and angelic activity around the throne.

Revelation 8:7-13 records John's vision of the angel sounding the first four trumpets, hail and fire falling, a mountain cast into the sea, and a falling star.

Revelation 9 records John's vision of the angel sounding the fifth and sixth trumpets, including the angel with keys to the bottomless pit, locusts, an army of horse and other vivid images.

Revelation 10:1-7 records John's vision of a mighty angel clothed in a cloud with a rainbow on his head who had a little book.

Revelation 11:1-2 records John's vision of the temple measurements.

Revelation 11:3-12 records John's vision of the two witnesses, including their murder and resurrection.

Revelation 11:4 records John's vision of two olive trees and two candlesticks.

Revelation 11:7 records John's vision of the beast in the bottomless pit.

Revelation 11:15-19 records John's vision of the seventh trumpet sounding, the temple of God opening and the ark of the covenant, with lightnings, noises, thunderings and hail.

Revelation 12:1-2 records John's vision of a woman clothed in the sun, with the moon under her feet and a garland of twelve stars who cried out in labor and gave birth.

Revelation 12:3-6 records John's vision of a great red dragon with seven heads and ten horns.

Revelation 12:7-9 records John's vision of the war in heaven.

Revelation 13:1-10 records John's vision of the beast rising out of the sea with the name blasphemy.

Revelation 14:1-5 records John's vision of the Lamb of God on Mount Zion with the 144,000.

Revelation 14:6-7 records John's vision of angel with the everlasting gospel.

Revelation 14:8-13 records John's vision of an angel announcing Babylon's fall.

Revelation 14:14-16 records John's vision of the Son of Man with a sickle.

Revelation 14:15-20 records John's vision of an angel reaping the harvest, and the angel with authority over fire, and the great winepress of God's wrath.

Revelation 14:17-19 records John's vision of the angel coming out of the temple with a sharp sickle.

Revelation 14:18 records John's vision of the angel with power over fire

Revelation 15:1-8 records John's vision of the angels with the final plagues

Revelation 15:5 records John's vision of the temple of the tabernacle of the testimony of heaven opened.

Revelation 16:2 records John's vision of the plague that comes upon those who take the mark of the best

Revelation 16:3 records John's vision of the sea turning into blood

Revelation 16:16 records John's vision of angels with the seven bowls of wrath

Revelation 16:18 records John's vision of Babylon's destruction

Revelation 19:1-9 records John's vision of multitudes praising God

Revelation 19:11-16 records John's vision if Jesus riding a white horse

Revelation 19:17-21 records John's vision of an angel in the sun

Revelation 20:1-3 records John's vision of Satan being bound for one thousand years

Revelation 20:1-10 records John's vision of thrones of judgment, resurrection and Satan being loosed

Revelation 20:11 records John's vision of the God's white throne

Revelation 20:12 records John's vision of the book of life opened

Revelation 20:14 records John's vision of death and hell

Revelation 21 records John's vision of the New Jerusalem

Revelation 22:1 records John's vision of the river of life

Revelation 22:2 records John's vision of the tree of life

CONCLUSION

YOU CAN READ these activations over and over and see something different every time. You may also take the principles of the activations in the section on parables, names of God, visions and Bible scenes to do your own activations that are not in this book.

Don't wait for the Lord to ask, "What do you see?" Begin actively to ask Him to show you what He sees. Follow Jesus' instructions in Matthew 7:7 (AMPC): "Keep on asking and it will be given you; keep on seeking and you will find; keep on knocking [reverently] and [the door] will be opened to you." Part of honing any spiritual gift is exercise and hunger.

Pray this prayer with me right now:

Father, in the name of Jesus, give me a hunger to see in the spirit the things You want to show me. Open my eyes and help me see the angelic dimension, the secret places in Your Kingdom, wicked counsel of the enemy, the secrets of men's hearts, visions like Ezekiel saw and more.

Help me sanctify my eyes so that I do not see worthless things that cloud my vision. Teach me to walk circumspectly in the seer gift. Purify my heart so that my motives stay in line with Your kingdom. Teach me to see.

ABOUT THE AUTHOR

JENNIFER LeCLAIRE is an internationally recognized author, apostolic-prophetic voice to her generation, and conference speaker. She carries a reforming voice that inspires and challenges believers to pursue intimacy with God, cultivate their spiritual gifts and walk in the fullness of what God has called them to do. Jennifer is contending for awakening in the nations through intercession and spiritual warfare, strong apostolic preaching and practical prophetic teaching that equips the saints for the work of the ministry.

Jennifer is senior leader of Awakening House of Prayer in Fort Lauderdale, FL, founder of the Ignite Network and founder of the Awakening Blaze prayer movement.

Jennifer formerly served as the first-ever editor of *Charisma* magazine. Her work also appeared in a Charisma House book entitled *Understanding the Five-Fold Ministry* which offers a biblical study to uncover the true purpose for the fivefold ministry and *The Spiritual Warfare Bible*, which is designed to help you use the Bible to access the power of the Holy Spirit against demonic strongholds and activity. Some of Jennifer's work is also archived in the Flower Pentecostal Heritage Museum.

Jennifer is a prolific author who has written over 30 books. Some of her materials have been translated into Spanish and Korean.

Beyond her frequent appearances on the Elijah List, Jennifer writes one of *Charisma*'s most popular prophetic columns, *The Plumb Line*, and frequently contributes to *Charisma*'s Prophetic Insight newsletter. Her media ministry includes her website; 500,000 followers on Facebook, Twitter and YouTube. Jennifer has been interviewed on numerous media outlets including USA Today, BBC, CBN, The Alan Colmes Show, Bill Martinez Live, Babbie's House, Atlanta Live and Sid Roth's *It's Supernatural*, as well as serving as an analyst for Rolling Thunder Productions on a *Duck Dynasty* special presentation.

Jennifer also sits on the media advisory board of the *Hispanic Israel Leadership Coalition*.

Jennifer is affiliated with:

- *Network Ekklessia International (NEI),* an apostolic network founded by Dutch Sheets
- *Forerunner Ministries*, founded by Ken Malone
- Bill Hamon's *Christian International Network*

- Chuck Pierce's *Apostolic Network: The United States Coalition of Apostolic Leaders* (USCAL)
- *The International Society of Deliverance Ministers*

Jennifer has a powerful testimony of God's power to set the captives free and claim beauty for ashes. She shares her story with women who need to understand the love and grace of God in a lost and dying world. You can also learn more about Jennifer in this broadcast on Sid Roth's *It's Supernatural*.

OTHER BOOKS BY JENNIFER LECLAIRE

Angels on Assignment Again

Decoding Your Dreams

The Seer Dimensions

Walking in Your Prophetic Destiny

Victory Decrees (devotional)

The Spiritual Warrior's Guide to Defeating Water Spirits

Releasing the Angels of Abundant Harvest

The Heart of the Prophetic

A Prophet's Heart

The Making of a Prophet

The Spiritual Warrior's Guide to Defeating Jezebel

Did the Spirit of God Say That?

Satan's Deadly Trio

Jezebel's Puppets

The Spiritual Warfare Battle Plan

Waging Prophetic Warfare

Dream Wild!

Faith Magnified

Fervent Faith

Breakthrough!

Mornings With the Holy Spirit

Evenings With the Holy Spirit

Revival Hubs Rising

The Next Great Move of God

Developing Faith for the Working of Miracles

You can download Jennifer's mobile apps by searching for "Jennifer LeClaire" in your app store and find Jennifer's podcasts on iTunes.

GET IGNITED! JOIN THE IGNITE NETWORK

I BELIEVE IN PROPHETIC MINISTRY with every fiber of my being, but we all know the prophetic movement has seen its successes and failures. With an end times army of prophets and prophetic people rising up according to Joel 2:28 and Acts 2:17-20, it's more important than ever that we equip the saints for the work of prophetic ministry. Enter Ignite.

Ignite is a prophetic network birthed out of an encounter with the Lord that set a fire in my hearts to raise up a generation of prophets and prophetic people who flow accurately, operate in integrity, and pursue God passionately. I am laboring to cultivate a family of apostolic and prophetic voices and companies of prophets in the nations who can edify, comfort and exhort each other as we contend for pure fire in the next great move of God. My vision for Ignite covers the spiritual, educational, relational and accountability needs of five-fold ministers and intercessory prayer leaders.

You can learn more at: *www.ignitenow.org.*

AWAKENING PRAYER HUBS PRAYER MOVEMENT

THE AWAKENING PRAYER HUBS mission in any city is to draw a diverse group of intercessors who have one thing in common: to contend for the Lord's will in its city, state and nation.

The vision of Awakening Prayer Hubs prayer spokes is to unite intercessors in cities across the nations of the earth to cooperate with the Spirit of God to see the second half of 2 Chronicles 7:14 come to pass: "If My people, who are called by My name, will humble themselves and pray, and seek My face and turn from their wicked ways, then I will hear from heaven, and will forgive their sin and will heal their land."

For many years, intercessors have been repenting, praying, and seeking God for strategies. Awakening Prayer Hubs intercessors will press into see the land healed, souls saved, churches established, ministries launched, and other Spirit-driven initiatives. Blaze intercessors will help undergird other ministries in their city, partnering with them in prayer where intercession may be lacking. Although *Awakening Prayer Hubs* prayer spokes are not being planted to birth churches, it is possible that churches could spring up from these intercessory prayer cells if the Lord wills.

You can find out more about this prayer movement at: *www.awakeningprayerhubs.com*

You can also join the Awakening House Church Movement at: *www.awakeninghouse.com*

Or plant a house of prayer via Awakening House of Prayer.